PAUL SCHNEIDER
The Pastor of Buchenwald

1318501

CONTENTS

PAUL SCHNEIDER

PAUL SCHNEIDER

The Pastor of Buchenwald

A free translation of the
story told by his widow,
with many quotations from
his diary and letters

by

E. H. ROBERTSON

Schneider

S.C.M. BOOK CLUB
81 W. VAN BUREN STREET
CHICAGO, ILL.

*English Version by Rev. E. H. Robertson.
Title of the original German work: Der
Prediger von Buchenwald. Das Martyrium
Paul Schneiders. Copyright by Lettner-
Verlag, Berlin. Licensed English edition by
Student Christian Movement Press Ltd*

First published 1956

*Printed in Great Britain by
Northumberland Press Limited
Gateshead on Tyne*

1318501

CONTENTS

FOREWORD

PAUL SCHNEIDER was a simple German pastor of
the Reformed tradition. He was not brilliant and would
probably never have been known outside the small
circle of his friends if his integrity had not been tried on
a national stage. He was a man of integrity. Many more
brilliant men found reasons for co-operating with the
Nazis. Paul Schneider could not thus betray himself. His
letters and papers make no contribution to theology and
they tell us little we did not know about Germany in
the thirties; but his wife was right to collect them and
publish them with the story of his life. He was a simple
uncomplicated man and she saw the value of this record
of integrity. While I have been translating this book, I
have several times visited the Rhineland and entered
many studies and libraries. Always I found the little
black volume, *Der Prediger von Buchenwald* on their
shelves. Frau Schneider was right. We needed the record
of a man who fought Nazism for no other reason than
that he could not disobey Christ.

The German edition is a collection of letters and
papers, beginning with considerable comments and
explanations by Frau Schneider and gradually developing until less and less comment is needed, because the
letters tell their own story. I have kept that form,
although the book has been much reduced. Some of the
comments and some of the papers and letters have been
omitted because they are of interest largely to those
who knew Paul Schneider and his people. Other passages
have been cut simply because of size. On the whole, not

7

much is lost and I have tried not to omit any development in Schneider's thinking about his struggle. The
book is in fact by Paul Schneider and his wife added
only what is needed to understand the background to
the letters. She tells us only a little about her man, but
enough to commend his letters to us. Throughout the
book, when we are not reading Paul Schneider's papers,
we are listening to his wife. All the linking material is
by her. The only exceptions to these are where I have
found it necessary to make clear to an English reader
the use of certain German phrases or terms. Sometimes
I have departed from strict translation and paraphrased.
This is an effort to convey what E. V. Rieu called 'the
principle of equivalent effect'. It has allowed, for
example, the substitution of a fairly well-known English
hymn for a fairly well-known German hymn and the
alteration of the context accordingly. I have tried to
write in English what Paul Schneider would have written
if he had been an English pastor and the drama of his
challenged integrity had been enacted in an English
village. The German edition of the book had a foreword
by Prof. Dr Heinrich Vogel and I should like to endorse
his tribute by translating a passage from that foreword
and making it my own.

'A voice crying in the wilderness of the concentration camp, from among the downtrodden, the suffering
and the unprotected, himself the poorest of them all—a
voice from God—that was this Pastor Schneider, whom
we dared to call our brother.

'It is indeed wonderful to see, from this material
which his widow lays before us in this book, how carefully his life was guided and prepared. Almost everything that happened to him, we can now see as training
to make him ready and able to become "the pastor of
Buchenwald".

'When one of his fellow prisoners stood beneath his

window and pleaded with him to save himself and think
of his wife and children, he got a straight answer: "I
know why I am here." That was typical of the man. He
knew, with a certainty which triumphed over all
opposition, why he must walk in this way, as a good
shepherd to his flock, and witness, among the dying, to
the Lord Jesus Christ, even unto death. The true great-
ness of this man is seen when we recognize that he was
not compelled to walk this way of martyrdom. At least,
he was not compelled by any outward force. The walls
of his prison were made of—paper! That is to say, he
had only to sign a little piece of paper, promising to
give up the care of his church, and he would be allowed
to go free. So they would remind him, goading his
conscience, at every camp roll-call. Sign and go free!
He had only . . . It took more than an iron will to hold
on, despite the torment of the prison house; it took more
than courage to go through with it, when all the time
a way out was offered. It needed the grace of God. These
pages are brimful of the gentle light of that grace.
"Gentle", because his words are so unheroic, so human.

'We are grateful to the widow of this man for the
generous way in which she has allowed us to read her
personal letters; letters he sent to her from prison and
concentration camp. She was honoured to help bear his
burden and to share the dangers of his faithful witness.
The natural concern of the father and the husband in
these perilous times, which we meet constantly in the
letters, speaks volumes for the deep, unspoken anxieties
which were no small part of the burden these two brave
souls had to bear.'

For me, the translation of this book, which has been
with me at odd times for about nine months, has been
like taking a room in a strange house and among a
strange people. Anyone who has done that will know
how often we begin by wondering if we shall ever get

used to their ways and really know them. Then, after months or years, according to temperament, we wonder if there was ever a time when we did not know them. So it has been with me. I cannot remember now that once I did not know the man. The walls of Buchenwald, the manse at Dickenschied and the good people there now seem to be my lifelong friends. I have tried to remember that my readers do not yet live in this house among these strange people; but I hope that when they have read the book they will know and honour my friend, Paul Schneider, as well as his brave wife and their children.

EDWIN ROBERTSON

I

CHILD AND STUDENT

PAUL SCHNEIDER was born on August 29th, 1897. He liked to call himself a country parson's son and certainly his childhood in the village of Pferdsfeld (near Kreuznach), where his father was the protestant minister, deeply impressed on him a love of nature, an understanding of animals and a liking for country folk. The village of Pferdsfeld was his childhood paradise. At the age of 34 he had not lost the feel of it. In a letter, during a holiday there, written to his church in 1931, he says: 'Here, on this piece of ground where my cradle stood, where I received my first impressions of childhood, I am more than ever convinced that we do well to cherish our memories of home, to remember its customs and its love. This little town, high up in the meadow land at the opening of the valley, the powerful woodland, the humble old cottages, the little shops, the street corners, the people—many of them hardly changed since I was a boy—the splashing fountains, still the same. All these capture my soul with a good, strong love. My body and my soul rest quietly in the lap of home.' The bond was strong. 'The tie which binds us to our native hills,' he once wrote in his diary, 'may be overcome, but is never lost.'

Yet it would be wrong to assume from this that his childhood was untroubled. His father was in many ways a hard man. He preached the Law more often than the Gospel!

Paul's father was of the Reformed tradition, and his

family, like many Calvinists everywhere, were industrious tradespeople. An aunt, a teacher at the local girls'
school, brought Paul's father up and was to him both
teacher and spiritual guide. He never knew his mother.
The aunt brought him early under the influence of
Kohlbrügge and he was eventually confirmed by Pastor
D. Krummacher in the Reformed Church. Later he
studied Theology at Tübingen and was greatly influenced
by Professor T. von Beck. Thus Paul's father had a good
training; but he was slow and always seemed to be han-
dicapped in his ministry. The death of his wife turned
him completely on himself. From the shock of the
collapse of the nation in 1918, he never recovered. Only
very seldom could we young people catch a glimpse of
his true nature or come in contact with his restrained
goodness. As a girl, I was always astonished at his prac-
tical exegesis of the Scriptures, but I always felt that he
was better with the Law than with the Gospel!

Paul never failed in respect for his father, but there
is no doubt that his influence represents the darker side
of Paul's childhood. His father's austerity dug deep into
the boy's soul. The most memorable example of this was
an incident in the manse garden, where stood a goose-
berry bush which Paul was forbidden to touch. One day,
he lied to his father about it. He could never be sure in
later years whether he lied out of obstinacy or fear of
punishment. He never confessed to his father; but, so
austere was the atmosphere of that home and so fierce
the texts his father used about falsehood, that a shadow
lay over his life for years. He was constantly beset by a
sense of guilt. The boy grew up and became strong, but
the shadow had injured his soul. He longed for purity.
As late as 1925, that is, at the age of 28, when doubts
were attacking his faith, he wrote in his diary: 'Is this,
my present condition, the endless working out of the lie
in the garden at Pferdsfeld? Now comes the great

rejection, the great solitude. Oh that I had said then to my father, " Father, I have lied ". The lie to my earthly father has led me on to falsehood before my heavenly Father. Now I cannot find my God. Oh Lord, take not thy face from me! '

It was an added touch of harshness, or perhaps an attempt to heal, which led the father to give Paul as his confirmation text, John 18.37; Jesus said : 'To this end was I born, and for this cause came I into the world, that I should bear witness unto the truth. Everyone that is of the truth heareth my voice.'

This hard lesson, burnt in upon his soul, gave Paul a more than usual sense of truth. He would pursue it endlessly, long after others had given up. Even in his student days, he was more persistent than they all, questioning and examining statements and theories until he could accept or reject them. He wearied many in his pursuit, but never gave up. It was a long, hard way for him and for those who loved him; because it was a way he had to tread alone. Many of his colleagues have paid high tribute to his passion for truth; it led him at last to Buchenwald.

But, back to the manse at Pferdsfeld. There was also a brighter side to his childhood—his mother. Paul knew her only as an invalid. Her first two children were born dead and her own health began to deteriorate; but she bore three more sons. Paul was the second of them—the fourth child. His other brother was six years younger. Paul's mother had been an orphan from an early age and was brought up in the Orphanage at Mülheim/Ruhr. Later she became a teacher there. She had a happy nature, full of the joy of life, loving all beautiful things. Despite all her handicaps, she was able to give her children a happy childhood. She was always full of ideas for adventures and games. 'Mother's Christmasses' were for Paul, all his life, the best and happiest—the essence

of all that was lovely. 'She remained the happiest person
in our house,' Paul wrote, 'so long as she was with us.'
She became more and more of a cripple and was at last
bound to her chair. Even then she took part in the joy of
life and sang and talked as one who was in the main
stream, not as one watching from the bank. 'She remained the happiest person in our house.' She died in
1914. In 1918, Paul was still counting the Christmasses
'without mother' and recording his sorrow in his diary.

Paul went to school at Kreuznach for his secondary
education until 1911, when the family moved to Hochelheim, for mother's health, and Paul went to Giessen.
This was a much longer journey, but Paul was fourteen
now and a boy of energy and spirit. He went part of
the way by bicycle and part of the way by train. There
was a saying in the village that when the minister's son
set forth there was no safety on the road for anyone!
He soon became a legend. Paul finished at school in
1915 and wanted to study medicine. It was, however,
1915, and Paul gladly went to do his war service. He
was in his element as a lieutenant, first in the Cavalry
and then later with the Heavy Artillery. He was badly
wounded in the stomach. At the critical period of his
operation, he had a dream and said as he came out of
it: 'A fair wife and healthy children stand before me.
For them, I must get-well.' On the way back, he met a
girl from the Rhineland, whose pure and simple ways
profoundly affected him. He did not quickly recover
from this contact and, when he did, it was typical of
him that he was worried lest he had given the girl any
hope of their relation developing. He did not rest until
he had seen her and her family again and put all minds
at rest. This working woman later mourned with me the
'always honoured and beloved Paul'.

After the War, Paul gave up the idea of studying
medicine and with a clear call took up the training for

a minister, 'to heal the people'. Paul had already come
into contact with liberal theology at the school in
Giessen. A school friend wrote about this in a way that
illustrates his developing character and his passion for
truth. 'Ever since school days we had a very close
friendship, which was menaced almost to breaking point
by our discussions over a radical liberalism, which Paul
rejected. This happened at the Giessen Seminar, where
scarcely a day passed without a violent theological discussion. These discussions we had as we walked from
the University to the railway station and continued in
the train. Often Paul would forget his stop and I would
have to remind him to get off. He pursued his discussion
until the last possible moment, even on the footplate of
the carriage and almost always having to jump off as the
train left the station! Paul's passion for "the truth"
went to the uttermost limit and he would have sacrificed
his friendship if he held that to be necessary. But I
believe now that our struggles were a preparation for
his later struggles, which were pursued with the same
blazing honesty.'

Paul studied at Giessen and at Marburg. While at
Giessen, in 1919, the humiliation of Germany and its
complete collapse came home to him. He began to
interest himself, like all German students, in political
movements and their programmes for the future of
Germany. He was constantly concerned with Bolshevism
and Socialism. An entry in his diary about this time tells
of his opinion of these: 'Bolshevism is a contradiction
because it seeks to create a situation depending on love
and goodwill, one toward another, and it seeks to create
it by force. The violent creation of this situation can
never guarantee that those who take part in the revolu-
tion and the strikes, which are apparently necessary
preliminaries, will in fact have these virtues of love and
goodwill. The proletariat, we are told, must conquer

until all is "socialized". But this worthy object is only
an outer change, not in the hearts of the men who make
up the new society. Instead of the old tyranny, we have
the new; a lasting dictatorship of the proletariat, in
which nothing except the places of the people is
changed. Indeed, things may be worse because the new
rulers are not trained to rule. Civilize the people, make
men better, and then you will bring into being, almost
automatically, the Welfare State.'

From Giessen, Paul went for a term to Marburg and
then, in the spring of 1920, to Tübingen. It was difficult
to find rooms there and Paul asked if he could go to the
minister's house. There he was received as one of the
family and a large family at that! There he filled a gap
in the family. His quiet and earnest ways recalled the
theological student, the beloved son, who had fallen in
the War. One girl in the family watched him closely.
They went together, these two young people, every day
into the town : he to University and she to school. In
the afternoon they would meet near the school and take
a boat on to the Neckar. Whether they were gliding
along in a dream or letting the boat get into difficulties,
they were wonderfully happy. When he left Tübingen
he wanted to say something to her, but could not—it
was still too early.

Meanwhile, Paul was reading Heim's *Ethics* and was
greatly impressed. He saw his past life as vanity and
was deeply disturbed about the state of his soul; he
longed for the peace of God. He was back again in Marburg for the winter term of 1921 and, a few days before
Christmas, he learned something of that peace he
sought. A ray of eternal life entered his soul and he was
filled with a great joy. For some time, he lived on the
excitement of this experience. He was, at least, sure
now that God can send light into a man's soul.

About this time, Paul had difficulty with the student

organization known as Vingolf—a large Christian and temperance movement of great influence, to which his father had belonged. When first he entered this organization at Giessen, he had asked himself whether it was worth the time and money spent upon it. There were always conflicts, especially over the 'temperance clauses'. Paul was not greatly concerned either way, but agreed that some kind of reform was needed. The only importance this movement has for the story of the Pastor of Buchenwald is that he found it necessary to sever his connections finally in 1933 when it came under Nazi influence and introduced 'Aryan' clauses. His indifference to its conflicts at this time, that is in 1921, is shown by an entry in his diary: 'I am quite content to remain in connection with this influential union; but, at the same time, I should be quite happy to have the time and energy for other things.'

How troubled Paul was over problems of faith and life, how Idealism and Liberalism pierced all his beliefs, we can imagine. That he was never far from the precipice, he tells us himself, or rather he wrote at the time in a letter to his future father-in-law: 'Life is incomprehensible and limitless. It is greater than we are, and all our persistence and our power cannot help us against it. It does not rest until it has beaten us down and broken us to pieces. Life says, "not as you, but as I will". So, man takes up a quite different attitude to time. Through failure and death and emptiness, time flows on, through doubt and bitter hurt. Man makes his joy and gladness as he builds up again and this is the joy he has to get used to—the joy of rebuilding. It is this joy that makes him strong to resist the violence of life and never lose himself.' So will 'his wings continue to grow'. The scraps of power emerge from the whirlpool again and he hopes to God 'that he will fashion me once more into a whole man'. Paul wrote that in July 1921.

As he prepared for his examinations in February 1922, he wrote: 'The art of life must daily be learnt anew. Here we are never finished, never "over the mountain". Our life must be an eternal military service, always "at your post". Without this constant readiness, the Tempter would overcome us, we should lose our way and depression would lay us low. If you believe, you stand; watch well, lest you fall, lest you are already fallen down into the depths—I have perhaps had too little faith, stressing too much the care of the body. I have exercised discipline and yet not conquered myself or my wellbeing. I have sought health of body and soul too much on the surface and not first in the deep things, at the very source.' That was in his diary for February 1922. He continued to trouble himself about the proper balance of physical to spiritual work. Here, another diary entry: 'I am still a seeker, I still ask myself, how much time I should give to the gymnasium and to work with spade and axe. Always, when I think I have a proper balance, I find that I have lost it again. Can God not give me all the strength I need, all the strength he wills, and throw this proper balance on the rubbish heap? Now, let this be my way, my life laid entirely on God, who, above reason and all this talk of a "proper balance", is all powerful and all good. I will let him say what I must do, how I must live, and I shall renounce all proper balances. My God, show me my way, the purpose of my life and my work. For this purpose he will make available to me all the strength I need for his service and much that now is dark will then become light. Send me, my God and Father, this liberating vision.' After his examination, this entry: 'I believe that I must work truly, industriously and carefully, but whether I succeed I leave to God.'

II

THE PREPARATION

ON APRIL 10th, 1922, Paul Schneider wrote of his plans for the final preparations before taking a pastorate of his own: 'First, I must get to know the workers and to do that I must take a job in a mine or factory. I am going to Dortmund. There in my own body I shall feel the trials and privations of the worker and perhaps discover into what corner of their heart religion has crept. I know too that as I work beside them, I shall learn to love them more.'

So, Paul went to Dortmund, into the heart of the industrial world. It was his first contact with this new world. Not only was it a new and grander landscape; but he began to feel that the men also were made from a quite different mould. He experienced here, too, his first clash between capitalism and socialism and was deeply impressed. His heart was with the workers; but all his upbringing until now had been conservative.

Paul had an uncle at Aplarbeck, which is a suburb of Dortmund, who was the director of a factory there. He offered Paul a good and well-paid job. This privilege troubled Paul, as we can see from an entry in his diary on the Thursday after he knew of the special job he was going to do among the miners. 'I cannot bring myself to accept this easy entry into the world of work. I will tell the works' manager that such a job would ill serve my purpose in coming here. I shall find work elsewhere.' So, true to his nature, Paul turned down the soft job. He sought work as other men did, tramping round the

19

town, and, after eight days, he found it. He became the
third man in a gang of workers at a blast furnace. He
lived in a working men's hostel and learnt to know the
different types of workmen. He shared their hardships
and their need. He learnt how terribly dear at this time
were the very necessities of life. His comment on the
industrial world, as he wrote it in his diary, is revealing.
'The organization is vast, industry is overpowering and
men are very small. Here is the trial by fire, to test
whether you are a man. The man who masters industry
must be as strong as a giant.' This was his first im-
pression. Now, he was a worker among workers. Yet
this experience did not lead him to a fuller understanding of the workers or a comradeship with them at once.
What he sought evaded him and his Christian message
seemed even more irrelevant as he pursued his difficult
way. He learnt the worth of a cup of cold water and a
bath at the end of a day's hard and hot work; but he
found it much more difficult to learn what relation his
Christian message had to the everyday work of his comrades. Gladly he joined his comrades in those outings
that broke the monotony of the dull work; but, return-
ing to his diary, he confessed his failure: 'Although I
am afraid to wander alone, I am driven to the discovery
that no one shares my interests. Loneliness frightens me
and the company of men also frightens me. I have
nothing more. All is a problem to me. Capitalism and
socialism, religion and life. I face nothingness, complete
and absolute emptiness. My working time is nearly
ended and I shall have to preach again. What shall I
preach? Power from on high fails me and I must, therefore, pray for power.'

He returned home; but, as he says, 'with very mixed
feelings'. Despite his failure to find men who shared his
interests and despite all his loneliness, he had developed
a comradeship with these men and they had accepted

him. On his last night, he tells us, they stayed up half the night bidding him farewell and, in the early morning, brought him to the train. They were genuinely sorry to see him go. He could find no adequate words to express his thanks, not even in the confidence of his diary; but he confesses that the time 'had strengthened my faith in our people and especially in our working people'. He never forgot their last words to him. It was the greatest of compliments: 'You are one of us. Try to stay like that.'

He left the industrial world in September 1922 to return home and help his father in Hochelheim. A month later, we became engaged at Weilheim, near Tübingen. Then followed a year of training for the ministry at the college in Soest. Here he came powerfully under the influence of the writings, especially the dogmatic writings, of Schlatter. With this influence his emphasis moved away from liberal theology to something resembling fundamentalism. Schlatter helped him to recover his message. He now had something positive to say again. His period of nihilism was over and he owed this largely to the quiet of Soest and the inspiration of Schlatter. This process was not easy. His diary tells of his first disappointment when he discovered that Schlatter was to be studied at the Soest college. He had read him before and thought he had had enough; but gradually he saw the gems in this conservative writer and confessed himself more conservative (or positive as he calls it) than liberal. Something of his struggle is seen in this entry: 'What the human heart finds most difficult is courage. He has courage who is completely set free from himself and only he has it. We must learn to hate ourselves. The darkest hours of our life also lead us nearest to God and we should be grateful to him for them.'

Paul never forgot the industrial world and even

while he studied in the quietness of Soest, he followed
the struggles of the workers in the Ruhr with great concern. 'We students,' he wrote, 'stand on the touchline
when the great game is played. We are free. We feel
nothing of the violence of this world or the fear of
unemployment. We are cared for by the State, by that
State with which this working community has to
struggle. Our conscience is burdened.' He saw that this
struggle of the workers might lead to a Welfare State
and he expressed his hopes in a letter about that time:
'The common suffering of the workers accounts for a
solidarity over the whole of Germany, welding them
together so close that they will build a workers' state,
which will then be fashioned into a Welfare State. It is
clear who can give the true power to the will of the
workers. This Welfare State owes more to the legitimate
longings of Christians than most popular movements
have yet realized.' He was not always as clear as that in
his support of popular movements, although he never
forgot the workers. He could write also with sorrow and
little hope in this world: 'A dark shadow lies over all
our lives and especially, my dear father, over the even-
tide of your life. Our beloved land is sore distressed,
spiritually troubled. In the storm and the breaking up
of the day, we have no anchor that holds.' His hope is
not in social reform any longer: 'But we have our
citizenship. And we know that despite all appearances,
it is our world which will triumph and, therefore, in
sorrow we are glad.' This was a period in which Paul's
social conscience was not silenced, but his confidence
derived from heaven, where truly his citizenship was.

At the end of October, he took his second theological
examination at Coblenz.

III

PREACHER AND PASTOR

As soon as Paul Schneider had finished his training he fled to Berlin by the cheapest means and found great satisfaction in the Mission to which he became attached. Both his own father and his future father-in-law were worried, because he seemed to be unsettled. They would both have preferred him to settle down more quickly to the ordinary ministry. Paul saw the danger; but he also saw the value of this work to his own spiritual development. It was not until the following summer, 1924, that he settled down. He made the decision during a holiday at home, when he saw how much his father needed help. For four months he remained in Hochelheim as a personal assistant to his father. He had plenty of opportunity for preaching and it was during these months that he learned the value of the regular ministry. He has some wise words to say about preaching regularly to a congregation in a letter he wrote about this time from Hochelheim: 'Here I can learn the art of preaching and have almost weekly opportunities for practice. Having to prepare a sermon every week makes me develop my thoughts and think through again many of the ideas I thought I knew well. Last week's sermon gave me a great deal of joy. It is now clear to me that it is absolutely necessary to think through the text and study its background carefully. Conversion alone is not enough to make a preacher. Now, I wonder that I was ever able to get involved in talking about the meaning of conversion or methods of evangelism.'

23

Paul was ordained early in 1925, before taking up an assistant pastorate in Essen-Altstadt. He was ordained in Hochelheim by the Superintendent. His text was from Rom. 1.16: 'I am not ashamed of the Gospel of Christ; for it is the power of God unto salvation, to everyone that believeth.' It did not go easily for him in this industrial parish. The work profoundly depressed him in soul and body and many a time he was on the verge of running away from his calling. A page from his diary will be enough to show his struggle: 'What is it that drives me out from my vocation? Is it a longing for ease, laziness or indolence? Or is it a love of adventure, a lack of persistence, or even a lack of character? I ought to be able to overcome this inability, this unwillingness to do my work. But haven't I tried and started afresh a hundred times? Are we Schneiders all unreliable, as a kind of reaction to the atmosphere in which we were brought up and which we can never get free of? My head is weak and my conscience, my will, is wavering and uncertain. I have preached the "pure Gospel" and lost my faith in Christ. I stand in the highest calling and yet only badly, if at all, do I live up to it. It seems to me that I have lived a great pretence, a lie. If thy Spirit, O God, had not constantly held me, I should long since have been lost. All that I say is mere words, carefully learnt and repeated a hundred times. I will not tolerate this division in myself any longer. Easter is over and the faithful congregation must lend me their faith in the risen Christ, that I might preach to them. Once again only the "broken cisterns" are mine. O God, thou seest how utterly dependent I am on thy grace alone. Have mercy upon me.' Such phrases recur throughout the pages of his diary at this time; but there are also times of joy in his work and these light up some of the darker pages.

After about a year in this industrial parish, he was

looking for a change of pastorate; but the death of his father brought matters to a decision. It was after a trial preaching in Kreis Wetzlar that he returned home to find his father dying. He had a stroke during the service. Three days later he died and Paul was unanimously elected his successor. So he became the pastor of Hochelheim. He knew how difficult was the task that lay ahead and he was troubled by the mixed motives in the invitation. Sentimental reasons are no substitute for spiritual ones. In his father's parish many found it easier to call him Paul than Pastor. He was called for mixed motives. Some wanted to have things just as they had always been, just like the old pastor. That meant, they didn't want to be disturbed, except perhaps by an occasional challenging sermon. Others, however, remembered how the young Paul had given a daring, liberal lecture to the sports club and hoped that he would stir up things a bit. Everybody wanted to fashion Paul in their own way. Small wonder that, from the very first day, there was tension.

Before Paul could settle, however, it was necessary to get the house decorated and prepared. While he waited, he served as assistant pastor in Rotthausen, not far from Essen. And then came our wedding. It was a time of beauty and early joy. Together, we prepared ourselves in the freedom and beauty of a new land. Our honeymoon was spent at Lake Constance and Oberstdorf. In the September, Paul was inducted by the Superintendent, who gave to him the very appropriate text from I Chron. 28.20: 'And David said to Solomon his son, Be strong and of good courage, and do it; fear not, nor be dismayed: for the Lord God, even my God, will be with thee; he will not fail thee nor forsake thee, until thou hast finished all the work for the service of the house of the Lord.' Paul preached a faithful sermon from the texts, I Tim. 3.1 and II Tim. 3.14-17.

Now, what of the Hochelheim parish? It includ
two villages, one with a population of 1,000 and anoth
of 500. They were mostly country folk, living close
their work. Here the famous Mainz cheese was mac
at first by hand in the separate houses, but later chee
factories grew up. During our time there, these fa
tories were already changing the character of the peop
Before motorized transport carried the produce of t
factories to the towns, the village women would car
their cheese to the big cities of Hesse and the Rhinelar
The constant travelling and their traffic with men of
kinds gave them a ready tongue, but it gave them al
a strong family sense. They were so often travelling th
the family festivals became for them great occasion
when they could sing their love songs. One of t
commonest is: 'Gladly, gladly, I come home—for the
is my heaven on earth.'

Paul grew daily in his pastoral office and only rare
now did his diary record his doubts and struggles. l
came to trust more and more in the power of prayer. l
fought his battles on his knees in his own room. Yea
after he said of prayer, in a sermon on Daniel, wor
which at this time he was learning. 'Prayer makes m
of us, men who bow only to God and confess him befc
the world. Prayer is the power of God needed to fig
the battles of life and of faith.'

Paul's chief concern in his pastoral work was for t
sick. He saw that often the spiritual illness was great
than the physical. He took great care to awaken the
conscience and to help them die. One dying you
woman said of him: 'One thing more I must say to yc
A happy dying hour is greater than the whole of li
That is what Pastor Schneider has taught me and w
dare question it?' Another incident is described by o
deaconess: 'I remember a young epileptic, who had
very bad attack, which lasted three days and thr

nights. His body was so fearfully distorted that, apart from the doctor, we all stood helpless around his bed and, despite the use of strong narcotics, we could not give him rest. The devil grinned at us from this helpless lad. Then Pastor Schneider came in and he soon had us all on our knees praying for the mercy of God. He took the sick lad in his arms and, what the nurse could not do, he did as he spoke gently to him and gave him rest and sleep. So often he had come like that. At nights when I stood by the sick bed and longed for help in my doubtful mind, I would hear his motor-cycle and in he would come to the sick-room, saying, "I knew I was needed here", and indeed he was in the truest sense of the word. When the young man came to die, it was with a clear mind that he faced the end of life. He sat up in bed and said: "I thank you all for everything; but that I can die at peace and with no fear of the dark grave— for that I thank our pastor! Now I am at peace with my God and the devil has no power over me." He laid himself down and died quietly and peacefully in Pastor Schneider's arms.'

He was a true pastor to his people and could talk to them quite bluntly when occasion required. For example, he went once to see a drunkard and sat with him and his family until well into the night, trying to reform the man. At last he said: 'You're a scoundrel.' When the man protested, he would have none of it, but persisted: 'Yes, you are a scoundrel and there is little chance of you getting any better until you say to me, Pastor, you're right, I am a scoundrel.'

Paul's pastoral care seemed infinitely patient: he never despaired of any. Yet he was not without trouble, particularly over the ancient customs of the Church. He tried to put meaning into conventional rites. One custom particularly troubled him. It concerned the Communion Service. Each age group would go to Communion on its

own particular Sunday, twice in the year. The festival
dress of the women gave to these Sundays a special
character and every one who came new to it was deeply
impressed by the ancient custom. But Paul knew the
temptation in this custom, especially to the young
women, to regard the Communion Service as a frivolous
and secular occasion. It assured that people came to
Communion; but where was the awe, the consciousness
of sin, the repentance, the preparation or any of those
things which Christ himself intended? These people
came on few, if any other, occasions under the Word of
God. Paul wanted to give meaning to this most holy
occasion. Older ministers whom he knew advised him
to leave the old customs and to use them as opportunities
for evangelism. But, as Paul said, these occasions were
so bedecked that they made evangelism well-nigh
impossible. As pastor, did he not share their responsibility when they came so lightheartedly to the Lord's
Table? Paul was particularly worried about the younger
groups. Even when they came lightheartedly to their
own Communion Service, he used the occasion to call
upon them to prepare themselves, asking them to come
forward and repent before they took the bread and
wine. Their lack of response, or, as he said, their lack of
courage led him to a decision. He would no more hold
the service as it had been held these past seven years. He
would require assurance from his young people that
they had prepared themselves adequately. His elders did
not agree with him. Nonetheless, without the consent of
his elders, he called a Church Communion for the last
Sunday in Advent, inviting his younger members to it
personally. He would end this secular festival and
dressing up of the young people. In a letter at that time,
he gave his reason: 'I can no longer encourage this
Youth Communion Service which has been the custom
here for seven years now. This Christmas, I could not

hold it in the old way. It was nothing but a disturbance, linked with sport and Hitler service. Worship of God had become a residue, a convenience, denying true service. Now, I have brokeen the custom. I have called for a Communion Service at which all members will confess their faith, coming to obey the Lord's command and for no other reason.' The congregation did not take this decision lying down. A small group of young and old let their protest be known. Anyone who knows anything of village life, the love of old customs and their close connection with new clothes, will know what a difficult task Paul had undertaken. One of his six elders took part in the opposition. This was Paul's last Communion Service at Hochelheim. He had gone too far in acting without the consent of his elders; but he had reckoned on their understanding of what he was trying to do in restoring a spiritual meaning to the Communion Service. But the right of the pastor to exercise discipline and the extent of that discipline was an old dispute. It had troubled Paul's father, who had strictly enforced the church discipline that excluded sinners from the Communion Service, until they had shown signs of repentance and an amended life. Paul could not always enforce the discipline as strongly as his father could, nor was he always clear about how far he should go. He was still young and this action had estranged him from some of his elders. This struggle over the secular Communion Service had important consequences for Paul. It prepared him for his future struggle with the Nazis. For the time, however, he was disturbed at the breach with his elders. While he sought unity with his elders, he could not deny his principles and he feared for the threat to church discipline. Calvin had said: 'Church discipline is like the sinews of the Church. If these sinews are cut, the whole body is without strength.' Paul sought, now with the co-operation of his elders, to exercise the

Church's discipline over any who openly broke one of God's holy ten commandments and thereby brought scandal upon the Church. Many of his congregation accepted this as right; but there was opposition to it. Let me give an example. A dispute between two members had reached such a pitch that the pastor intervened. He invited both of them to meet him in the vestry and give him an opportunity to reconcile them. He asked them to come a little before the Communion Service. One came, the other refused. Despite a refusal to accept this invitation, which clearly meant a refusal to be reconciled, he came to the Communion Service. Now he was a very influential man in the village. The pastor saw him at the service and sent word by the sidesman, asking him to leave the church, before the Confession. He remained. The pastor hesitated no longer. After the General Confession, he turned towards him personally and left no doubt that he expected a personal confession. The man stood up and went out.

In many other ways he followed the ancient custom of exercising discipline over those who did not bring a right mind to the Lord's Table. Paul took his pastoral work most seriously and was uncompromising in his principles. Especially he rebuked those who broke their marriage vows. He saw his task as pastor, especially in Hochelheim, quite clearly and fearlessly. Naturally, this brought him many enemies, especially among the young Nazis. Because of this, the local party leader watched Paul's attitude to the Nazi State with careful attention, putting every word and action under a strong magnifying glass.

Meanwhile, Paul's work among the young people grew. He tried every means to win new members from among the girls and boys of the village. He was happy in this work, playing with them at their sports, rambling over the hills with them and, above all, singing with

them. Of course, he did not forget Bible study, which
was the basis of all his work. Yet, he was up and down
in his work. Often we would say to ourselves, 'too
much attempted, too little achieved'.

I was happy in both the villages with the work among
the women. I remember it always with joy. These
women stood by us in all our difficulties and they were
the saddest when we left.

There was no thought of leaving in 1932 when Paul
and I threw ourselves into the manifold duties of his
pastorate. He had little time for politics in his busy life
at this time; but there is one circular letter, written in
1932 to the congregation, in which he expresses his
disquiet. After describing a great bicycle race in which
most of his young men had taken part, he continues:
'For the rest, I am disturbed by the way these strange
figures in yellow racing suits, quite unrecognizable to
their pastor, are greeted by the children and the other
excited Hitler girls with the typical "Heil" greeting.
This modern, popular movement—I must be careful not
to split my little flock with political divisions—but this
popular movement doesn't please me; I prefer the good
old ways of Christian service. Truly and openly, I have
given my support to Hindenburg and our vote has
shown our support for him; but his latest actions (i.e.
his support for Hitler) I cannot agree with. This disagreement aggravates my relation with the local Nazi leaders
—O this unholy Party Spirit! It is a sin against all the
people, both high and low. Where are the critical,
Christian judgments which will derive the rules for
political action, neither from nationalism nor from
socialism, but from the gospel? National Socialism does
not yet draw its strength from this source. Will it ever
do so? Is it really able to unite the two opposite poles
of nationalism and socialism and can it lead our people
to face that thorough religious renewal which they so

sorely need?' In February 1933, he wrote to one of our members who was seriously ill: 'To-day, a German evening with a German dance. Is that some special kind of dance, different from the usual? But to lectures and Bible study, we invite the majority of the people in vain. What has become of our protestant congregations? Yet these are God's times and somehow God will work among us. Hold fast to that and go forward gladly with faith.' In the village, National Socialism made slow headway. Many stood aloof, while the new Nazi ruler of the village was strongly criticized. One workman spoke out and his saying was often repeated: 'The only National-Socialist here is the pastor, and he's not one!' But when, on 1st May, 1933, all the people came together, encouraged to do so by many radio exhortations, and brought their gifts and offerings to the large camp service, Paul was filled with joy. He began to trust Hitler's 'social intentions'. He saw, however, that the Church had more to do than support this nation-wide collection for the poor. 'If all we can do as a Church,' he said, 'is to bring our collections like the rest and have no offering to bring for the inner renewal of our people, we are guilty of failure in our duty to God.' On the other hand, the constant ringing of the bells for national festivals, the formation of youth groups outside the Church, these and many other things worried him. He refused to use the 'German greeting'. The Aryan clauses, discriminating against Jews, troubled him and he refused to let them operate in his Church affairs. The 'German Christians', with their insistence on 'positive' teaching and their support for National Socialism, puzzled him. He attended one of their rallies in Frankfurt in the middle of July 1933 and there he made up his mind. He heard much with which he agreed about the need to build up the congregation and the means to strengthen lay witness. He was not satisfied, however, and records

that he found 'all was not well there' and that he feared
'that the truly positive wing of the German Christians
could not long remain in company with the rest if they
were to accomplish their intention.'

Towards the end of August his mind became clear.
He renounced the prefix 'German'. No Christian, he
told his congregation, no Christian who has repented
and known the forgiveness of Christ, has need to put
any 'German' in front of his honoured name. From this
moment, his position became clear and he never faltered
again.

In October, preaching in his branch Church at Dorn-
olzhausen, he protested against the accusation of bigotry
levelled at the Church by Röhm. Paul had expected
an official protest from the Church; but, when it did not
come, he took matters into his own hands. 'Röhm is
wrong,' he said, 'if he means that the "Third Reich"
can only be built with violence, or even if he means that
it can be built at all without an inner renewal of the
people.' Having made that protest, Paul went about his
work and was fully immersed in a singing festival when
the Superintendent Minister called for him. He took him
to Coblenz and there, before his superiors, he was reprimanded for his criticism. He had overstepped his
function, they said. The point was clearly made by the
bishop, who at that time was the leading German
Christian, the newly appointed Dr Heinrich Oberheid.
He explained to Paul that the attack by Röhm was
against certain political elements and had nothing to do
with the Church. Paul was for the time persuaded, or
as he said later, misled. He openly withdrew his protest.
The local Nazi leaders were not satisfied with the public
withdrawal. They regarded Paul, perhaps rightly, as a
dangerous man, and they watched his every step. This
inevitably made his pastoral work difficult and, added
to his disagreement with his elders over the festive

B

Communion Services, soon made it impossible for him
to stay in Hochelheim.

Goebbel's statement on 'Morals' was the immediate
cause of the break. It appeared in all the newspapers
and Paul felt compelled to protest against it. Other
difficulties followed fast and he was asked to give notice
that he would leave Hochelheim. His last protest in
Hochelheim against the German Christians was made
in a sermon on 'The Storm on the Lake'. He likened the
ship where Christ and his disciples were to the Church
of Jesus Christ. Here is his own report of that sermon:
'Whether I generally bring church politics or secular
politics into the pulpit, in that sermon I spoke strongly
against the German Christians. I had to because I saw
the danger to my people and the danger which threatens
the Church of Jesus Christ, as it rides like a ship through
the storms of this Third Reich.'

He felt that he had his people behind him; but he
obeyed when the order came to move to Dickenschied.
It was no longer possible to remain in Hochelheim. He
left on 25th April, 1934.

IV

DICKENSCHIED

1318501

PAUL SCHNIEDER was called to the church at
Dickenschied, 125 miles from Hochelheim. The whole
congregation, headed by the church warden, welcomed
the Schneider family as they arrived with all their furniture in a lorry and Paül shepherding it, like a faithful
sheepdog, on his motor-cycle. It was a truly happy welcome, matched only by the equally festive welcome at
the branch church at Womrath.

It was in Womrath he had his induction service.
Womrath, with its 500 inhabitants, unlike Dickenschied,
is almost entirely protestant. There on 8th May, 1934,
the village hung with church flags, amidst real rejoicing,
Paul was inducted as the minister of these two
congregations—at Womrath, a protestant church in a
protestant village; at Dickenschied, a protestant church
in a largely catholic village.

The Superintendent preached from Jer. 15.19-21:
' Therefore thus said the Lord, if thou return, then I will
bring thee again, *and thou shalt stand before me*: and
if thou take forth the precious from the vile thou shalt
be as my mouth: let them return unto thee; but return
not thou unto them. And I will make thee unto this
people a fenced, brazen wall; and they shall fight against
thee, but they shall not prevail against thee: for I am
with thee to save thee and to deliver thee, saith the Lord.
And I will deliver thee out of the hand of the wicked,
and I will redeem thee out of the hand of the terrible.'
That passage was chosen with care to meet the need of

the times and it proved an appropriate word of assurance for Paul Schneider. In particular, he and his friends
remembered that little phrase in verse 19, which is ren-
dered in England, 'and thou shalt stand before me', but
in German, 'und sollst mein Prediger bleiben', literally
'and thou shalt remain my preacher'. He remained
God's preacher and pastor even unto death.

The departure from Hochelheim had been a sad one,
but it was the price of peace. Yet this dearly-bought
peace at Dickenschied did not last long. It was broken
on 11th June, 1934. Here is how Paul describes the incident: 'I had gone over as a substitute to conduct a
funeral service in the small neighbouring town of
Gemuenden and it was at the grave-side that the incident
occurred. A giant parade had been called with bands
and colours and all the paraphernalia of the Nazi
organizations, especially the Hitler Youth, who were
much in evidence. The reason appeared to be that the
man I was burying had been a prominent leader of the
Hitler Youth. After the opening prayers, several
mourners brought wreaths and laid them round the
grave, sometimes making long speeches. There was a
certain religious content in these speeches at first; but
they gradually became less Christian. The deputy leader
of the work camp had already assumed a knowledge of
the fate of the deceased, which only God could know,
when the local Nazi leader declared that he would now
enrol the deceased in the Storm Troops of heaven. He
even named the famous Horst-Wessel detachment! I
had not yet pronounced the blessing and I saw myself
in danger of giving my blessing to this heavenly "Horst-
Wessel detachment". As reasonably as I could, I
asserted the Church's rights and declared her teaching:
"I don't know if there is a Horst-Wessel detachment in
heaven," I said, "but God, the Lord, bless thy going out
and thy coming in, from this time forth and for ever

more. Now let us go into the House of the Lord and hold the Memorial Service before God and his Holy Word." Thereupon, the local Nazi leader approached the coffin and, half addressing the crowd, half addressing the dead man, he said: "Comrade, whatever they say, you have gone home to the Horst-Wessel detachment." This had to be answered, so I said: "I protest. This is a church service and I, as minister, am responsible for the pure teaching of Holy Scripture." The parade was then marched off and did not attend the memorial service.'

Paul tried to discuss this personally with the local Nazi leader later; but he was already gone and Paul had to write his protest. It was a carefully worded letter and explained the nature of the funeral service.

Three days later, Paul was suddenly arrested and put in prison. No reason was given and he was kept in prison for a week. It was a mild imprisonment and visitors were allowed. Protests were signed in both his churches and public opinion was aroused. Many who had followed the Nazis began to waver. Their Christian faith was challenged by Nazism. Risking arrest themselves, many approached the local Nazi leader. He asked them if they would rather have their faith than National Socialism and when they answered Yes, he replied that they were not good Nazis. The village magistrate, father of one of the most prominent Nazis in the area, put the matter clearly when he said: 'As we have struggled for the Fatherland and for National Socialism, so we shall struggle for the faith of our Church.' The Fraternal of ministers also took action. A declaration was drawn up and read from their pulpits. Almost all his fellow ministers stood by him. They addressed a letter to the Minister of the Interior and the Vice-Chancellor to say that they stood solidly behind him in prison and under similar circumstances would so stand for the truth and if need be suffer. The Superintendent Minister, who lived

in the same town as Paul was imprisoned in, walked
through the centre of the town every day at noon,
openly carrying a packet to the prison with Paul's lunch.
The jailor made his prison as comfortable as he could
and I was allowed to visit him as often as I liked. After
six days, Paul was called before the judge and told that
the matter had been considered in Berlin and it was
decided that there was no case for punishment. However, he was warned 'not to adopt an antagonistic attitude to the State'. He was released. Two of his elders
came to bring him home and the whole congregation
gathered to rejoice at the safe return of their pastor.
Later, Paul wrote to the Commissioner of Police at
Coblenz to explain that he had no intention of adopting
'an antagonistic attitude to the State', but that his first
duty was to maintain the purity of Christian doctrine. If
there was to be peace between Church and State, he
said, it was essential that the Party should 'respect the
order, the doctrine and the outlook of the Church'. If
this were done, he assured the Commissioner of Police
that he would show due respect to the rights of the
State.

The year 1934 remained a troubled one. Paul described
it as a year in which it had been necessary 'to learn to
bear the tension'. So he wrote in 1st July, 1934: 'More-
over, trusting in God, we must learn to bear the tension
—and also learn to relax from the tension which is
everywhere about us, not in our congregations only, but
in our general relations with men—and to know that
the Church of Christ is rightly in a state of tension
towards the world when it returns to its normal life.
But may the Lord, whose little flock we are, make us
ready for the hour of decision when it comes, that we
may not deny him before men.' And again, the day after
his birthday, in the same year, he wrote expressing his
disapproval of the collaborating German Christians: 'I

also would like to wish myself a happy and peaceful new year of my life! Now, on the next few Sundays, we must certainly declare, on instructions from the Free Synod, our disobedience to the National Synod and its laws. This I do gladly, because I do not believe that we can ever achieve an honourable peace for the Church of Christ with these lying machinations. We indeed have need of God to care for us, not only outwardly, for wife and child, but also inwardly, to cleanse us and to give us courage and to equip us anew for his service and to be his witnesses. The only rebuke that we cannot endure is that we have cast away our trust in God. The world remains the world and our times are not more upright or more Christian than other times were. Yet will God renew his Church in these dangerous times and he will renew it in his own way, not as the German Christians think.'

That autumn, Paul, like many pastors, was dismissed and his stipend withdrawn. This gave to the Church an added responsibility. In Dickenschied, as elsewhere, collections were made for the ' poor pastor of Hunsrueck ' (the area in which Paul's church lay). The gifts were freely brought to the pastor's house, under the very eyes of the police, who strongly disliked the collection of goods and money for the pastor. Even those who were not churchgoers gave freely, because they felt a sense of solidarity with 'the needy, deposed pastor'. Within two or three months he was reinstated and received his stipend again. The struggle had been worthwhile. It gave the Church an opportunity to test its resources. Paul stood with those who believed in the churches being independent. He saw already that there was a state of war between Church and State, which could only be adequately dealt with if the Church depended not at all upon the State. He maintained this position to the end. Here already, in a letter of November 1934, he expresses his conviction: 'We must all get used to being in a state of war. Nor should we, as Christians, think that strange or out of the ordinary. Did not Jesus say, "I came, not to bring peace, but a sword"? And we as Christians can only truly love our people if we go back to the position outlined by Jesus. If we do not do that, we render our people and our State, as well as ourselves, only guilty service and we allow them to sink back into idolatry. Up till now, things have gone much too well for us. We have not yet suffered.' It was not easy, as Paul himself said in a letter a little later: 'It is costly to depend for the necessities of life entirely on the hand of God.' The struggle went on and Paul felt the strength of the Confessing Church growing in the Hunsrueck area. He tells us of his own experience in a letter of 22nd March, 1935: 'You will have heard about the 500 pastors arrested in Prussia as a result of last Sunday. They had refused to sign an order forbidding the circulation of the Manifesto of the Old Prussian Confessing Synod to the churches. It was hoped in this way to nip the movement in the bud and prevent its effective witness. The plan did not succeed. Too many pastors refused and too many were arrested. They were all set free at once. It was not so with us. I sat alone from Saturday evening to Tuesday morning in prison in Kirchberg, unfortunately the only pastor in the Hunsrueck. Still, it was good that one redeemed the honour of Hunsrueck. Apparently, all the other brethren in this area had been taken by surprise and gave their signatures not knowing what they did. Later they were very sorry and have since all taken their signatures back again; at least, all those who belong to the Fraternal. My wife had to suffer a house-searching on Saturday evening and I have still lost many papers and notes which were stolen on that night. They were, of course, looking for the copies of the Manifesto; but they were too late. I

had long since distributed them. The congregation
remains true. All this Holy Week I have had full services
every night. Last Sunday, of course, there was no service
because the pastor was in prison! It was not so bad
there in Kirchberg. Now I have made a fast friend of the
jailor, as the first Paul did at Philippi.'

Many friends came to see us during the spring and
summer of 1935. Hunsrueck is one of the loveliest
Rhineland areas and our visitors came to enjoy with us
its beauty. One visitor especially gave great joy. 'What
shall we make of this big boy?' said Paul. 'He doesn't
seem to notice the heavy storm clouds gathering. He
comes like the first ray of a beautiful morning after the
heavy days of rain.' It was good to see one more child
riding on his shoulder and laughing amidst the fears and
sorrows of the time. To his laughter and joy there
seemed to be no end.

We did not often talk of the fear that gripped my
heart. But one day we had a never-to-be-forgotten conversation. Two incidents made me speak. The one on a
footpath. We overtook a man who soon fell into conversation with Paul. I knew his method of using such
opportunities well to witness for his Lord. He seemed
to me then like a man who knew that he had not much
time left. Flames leapt up as out of a hidden fire. The
second incident was at the edge of the woods, where a
gypsy encampment was pitched. The men lay round the
fire. Paul went over to them and spoke to them with a
sense of intense urgency. Paul did this quite naturally,
without condescension, and placed before them the
decisive question of accepting Christ.

On the way back I used the moment we had alone to
ask him to be careful. He replied that he could only
promise not to seek martyrdom. But, whenever he was
called to witness, he must witness, because on earth
there is no other salvation for men than in Jesus Christ.

My heart sank and I began to speak about his wife and children. That moment I can never forget. We stood on the stone bridge which led over the water. He looked at me with an indescribable look, straight in the eyes, and said: 'Do you think God gave me my children only that I might care for their outward needs to keep them strong in body? Do they not depend on me also to care for their eternity? And my wife? Perhaps it is for you that I must suffer, perhaps in this way and in no other can you break through to true faith.' Silent and inwardly shaking we walked home. I can never forget.

The next Sunday was the day of my departure. It was Communion Sunday and all was ready in the church. By ancient custom, two elders came to the pastor's house to bring him to the Lord's Table and with him all that was needed for the service. The church lay at the other end of the village and they had to walk through the long village street. So they went that day, the pastor in the middle, dressed for the service and with the Bible in his hands. On his left hand and on his right hand walked the elders with the Cup and the Bread in their hands. Led away like that I saw him after our last meeting. It was like a frightening prophecy.

I knew then that he must continue in his fearless witness. These words of a friend completely describe his attitude, which from now on never wavered: 'He knows now that he serves his people, whom he loves, only when he declares to them the whole truth and the uncompromised gospel. He could not, therefore, be "a reed shaken by the wind", repeating what men wanted to hear or what was safe. He holds firm to this resolve, in season and out of season.'

Paul was never on holiday from his pastoral work. In the train and out walking, he would use every opportunity to get into conversation with people, forgetting his family, or at least putting them behind him.

Working in the fields was often a relaxation for Paul.
He would gladly throw himself into the work of harvest-
ing. His natural manner and his gift for understanding
the work of the fields brought him very near to the
farming people. Mowing the hay in the early morning
was his special joy. Already in his first pastorate, I can
remember someone coming to me with surprise and
saying: 'Once when I was driving through your parish
I saw something I could hardly believe. Pastor Schneider
was loading a wagon of hay! By the side of the road,
the woman who had found the work too heavy for
her was sitting with surprised eyes watching him.
Apparently, without stopping to think, Pastor Schneider
had jumped from his cycle and started loading the hay
on to the wagon.' It was just like him.

Paul was often rebuked in his church work for saying
things the Party might object to. He was always being
called to the mayor's office to be warned. In the winter
of 1935-6, I can remember twelve such occasions. He
was usually able to explain that what he had said was
not really as bad as the informers had reported; but the
special court recorded it and multiplied it against him.
On one occasion, he had made a collection for the Jews
—that referred to the Christian Mission to Israel; on
another occasion, he had called Hitler a 'devil'—what
he had really said was, 'whether Hitler be from God or
the Devil, only the future can tell'; and so on. The elders
stood firmly by their pastor and gave such strong warn-
ings to possible informers that there was a temporary
lull.

Then came the election of 1936. At that election, there
was no room on the ballot paper for a 'No', as there
had always been before. It was not a true election and
we, therefore, stayed in the house. Paul was not content
with this passive attitude. He saw the church decorated
with flags and heard the bells ringing, as is usual at

election times; but he feared this might be interpreted as the Church's blessing upon the election. Therefore, he published the following declaration:

'For this statement to the Evangelical-Reformed Church of Dickenschied, I hold myself solely responsible.

The apparent participation of the Church in to-day's General Election, by the ringing of bells and the display of flags, compels me to explain why I am taking no part in this day.

To the plans and affairs of the State, the Church can either give the blessing of God, or, if its action is directed against God's Will and Word, the Church can and must present the State with a divine warning.

The appearance of flags and the sound of bells can too easily be taken to mean that the Church gives its blessing. Such a blessing, the Church cannot give the State on this occasion. For clearly, this election asks not only that we should approve of the Führer and sanction his foreign policy. It concerns the fate of our nation and requires us to sanction the philosophy of National Socialism. Yet this philosophy becomes more obviously opposed to biblical Christianity every day.

The fate of Germany will not be decided by troops on the Rhine, but by the attitude of our people to the Word of God. That is why the question of philosophy and world attitude is at present more important than any other. More than ever to-day, the German people and especially the young people are openly estranged from the Church of Christ and the teaching of the Bible. That is why we must reckon with the possibility of a strong anti-God movement. We may well find a secular, non-Christian school forcibly replacing our own confessional school.

It is not the least important promise of responsible men in State and Party that they would do quite differently from what they now plan to do in these matters. Therefore, the Church of Christ cannot approve of the Third Reich in this most important question. It cannot give its blessing to this election for the new Party Reichstag. The Church would be more guilty than the Führer or the Government if it did not declare the warning of God and the judgment of God against this de-christianizing of our people.

But you, my dear congregation, must defend your faith, witnessing in this election also to the honour and majesty of the living God, the Father of our Lord Jesus Christ. Him you must declare against the idols and the lords of this passing world.'

Contrary to expectations, we were left alone on election day, apart from the usual party notices. On the Sunday, which was Easter Day, we saw painted opposite our house, in large red letters: 'He has not voted. Fatherland, People, what do you say??!!' Now the German people had no way of answering that question, but our congregation had. They did so quite definitely. Although it was Easter morning, they came with brushes and cleaning materials and festive energy and they wiped away the slogans. Later, when they came to service, Paul thanked them.

In July, 1936, we had our holiday with my mother in Tübingen. The cultural life of the town was at its height, with a Mozart Festival. Mother gladly joined in all this, but it was no relaxation for Paul. He came to please us. So, the first part was no real holiday for him and made our relation somewhat strained. How often I have wanted to put that right! We had a number of differences of opinion and later decided that he should have ten days away from Tübingen and away from Mother. Paul wrote to explain the reason for this in the kindest way. For the last four of those days I joined him. It was our last and happiest holiday together. A woman at our table in the guest house asked us: 'Are

you on honeymoon?' How delighted we were to reply:
'No, we have five children at home.' Paul retained his
capacity for happiness. This is well illustrated by a letter
he wrote to a teacher friend on 2nd September,
1936:

'How great a gift of God it is that, despite the heavy
clouds that hang over us and the dangerous times in
which we live and the uncertain way we in the Confessing Church must go, despite all this, we are happy,
I might almost say carefree. To God we owe our family,
our dear children, our daily bread, our office and all that
is dear to us. Here on the 23rd August, we have had the
Manifesto of the Confessing Church and of the Council
read out. It did my heart good. A sense of freedom came
to me as I realized that our Church leaders had found
this word and declared it. With this, we can push our
way through the fog of diplomacy and lies which
characterizes the present situation and bewilders our
poor people. Like the sun breaking through after weeks
of rain and anxiety about the harvest was this word
from God to me.'

One great concern of Paul's was the church schools.
In both his villages he had two single-class schools. He
regarded the children in these schools as his own special
concern (indeed, among them were our own children)
and grieved that they seemed to be so much affected by
the spirit of the times. In 1936 he wrote: 'We have
already had great difficulty with the education of our
children, because our schools are so badly endowed and
equipped. They learn very little because the teacher is
always so full of the new ideas and the new methods.
Now they have, both before and after school, a new
kind of prayer, which is neither Christian nor protestant.
These prayers breathe instead the air of faith in
Germany.' Both teachers did their best to twist the Bible
stories in accordance with the latest Nazi teaching. Paul

discussed with his elders the need for a separate class for the younger children, who were not yet old enough to be prepared for confirmation. This idea was later carried through by his successor. Paul worked out a detailed plan of instruction for it while he was in prison in 1937. It included Bible study, hymns and catechism questions, and these things were to be taught either at home or under the arrangement of the Church.

Before this plan had even formed in his mind, he tried to deal with the teachers personally. He was concerned for them as well as for their schools and felt it a pastoral duty to win them over to a better mind. They did not argue; they simply laid before him declarations of the Nazi party. The teacher of Dickenschied was especially hostile. He tried to lodge a legal complaint against Paul and, in the course of proceedings, the catholics, who constituted two-thirds of the village, became involved. Paul was particularly worried about this, because he had hoped to settle the matter within his own congregation. He explained his own attitude at the end of a protest written by his elders to the President. Here is what he wrote: 'It is a great sorrow to me that, because of this renewed enquiry, I must explain these things all over again and bring to the public gaze again things we have already explained as a result of the complaint made by the catholics. We are concerned not only with these things as such and in themselves, as I have already made clear in my letter of 15th February about the earlier complaint. We are concerned about the hindrance to a full Christian education, which our schools are designed to give to the children of our people. We are, therefore, asking the government to intervene in this dispute on the basis of this principle and thus help to secure a true confidence and a lasting one between our Church and our school. We have already tried to settle this matter ourselves, by inviting the teacher, as a member of the

Church, to appear before the elders and discuss a recon-
ciliation. It was in vain. We have no dislike of the
teacher and this complaint is not a result of spite. We
are concerned only with the right and Christian education of our children.' He went on to ask the government
again to use its influence so that the teacher might be
persuaded to work more closely with the Church and
secure a Christian basis for all the education given to
the children. He showed here his concern as a father and
as pastor. The issue troubled him greatly and many of
his sermons at that time dealt with the importance of
Christian education. One he preached in January 1937,
for example, before the sending of either complaint,
dealt with the story of the boy Jesus in the Temple.
In it, he said: 'We desire a Christian education. Therefore, my dear people, we have something to unlearn. We
have always been taught that when we talk of
"christian" education, we must write the word with a
small letter. We must learn to write it with a capital
letter, because it comes from Christ, from Christ himself. No little thing will change the structure of our
children's hearts. Yet, he asks nothing less than to
imprint himself on their hearts and souls. If he wants
that, he cannot be content with a fragment or a corner
of the heart; he cannot have "a place" there; he cannot
be satisfied with an alloted and carefully sealed-off
portion. My dear people, his claim on us and on our
children is total; he demands our whole life.'

The trouble with the two teachers and their un-
christian teaching led Paul to discuss church discipline
frequently with his elders. Two other matters caused
great annoyance to the Church in Womrath. There was
a man, who for a long while had turned his back on the
Church, who now, with threats and abuses, withdrew
his child from the Sunday School. This, Paul pointed out,
was a serious step, because he had had the child baptized

and thus promised to give him such Christian instruction
as the Sunday School provided. Paul tried to reason with
him, but it was of no avail. And then there was a party
member, who had also been indifferent to the life of the
Church. Now he was setting himself up as a judge of
the life of the Church. Paul was always arguing with
him. He sought constantly to interpret the pastor's
Christian concern in such a way as to bring him under
political suspicion. He learnt from his son what the
pastor was teaching in the confirmation classes and sent
a full account to a German Christian minister. He tried
constantly to gain influence in the town. In Dickenschied and Womrath, the elders decided to exercise
church discipline over these men, as well as the two
teachers, because they had refused to appear before
them to settle the disputes with the pastor. In Dickenschied, they withdrew the declaration on the first Sunday
because they feared the consequences; in Womrath, the
elders stood firm by their decision. Here is the text of
the declaration of church discipline: 'Dear Church
member. The elders have found it necessary for the first
time in our church to restore the ancient and long-
neglected practice of public Christian discipline calling
for repentance. It concerns three occasions on which an
open scandal has come upon the Church of Jesus Christ,
and which could easily grow into a serious damage to
the congregation if it were not dealt with according to
the teaching of our Lord Jesus himself (Matt. 18.5-20)
and according to the confession of our Reformed
Church (Heidelberg Catechism, Questions 83H), which
place it under the strict discipline of the Church. This
church discipline of the congregation will be exercised
with the power of Jesus Christ on the authority of his
command and of his promise. Christ said, "Whatsoever
thou shalt bind on earth shall be bound in heaven: and
whatsoever ye shall loose on earth shall be loosed in

heaven ". Mark well that he is truly saying, " If you use the key, then shall I also use it; yes, if you do it, it shall be truly done. What you bind or loose, shall be bound or loosed, without my binding or loosing—it is the same work, yours or mine; do your work and mine is already done." There we have the authority to retain or forgive sins. The church discipline of the congregation shall be exercised, not out of anger or out of hate, but out of love. The Reformers understood church discipline as a costly method of exercising their love upon a man. It was the way in which the congregation condemned sin and, in so far as they did this seriously, they hoped to bring the man to repentance. So it is both the sorrow of the congregation and the love which seeks the betterment of the unrepentant sinner.

When it is suggested that the exercise of church discipline awakens enmity and divides the unity of the congregation, then it is not church discipline that is being criticized, but the false peace and false unity of the congregation. There is no true unity or peace without truth.

1. Far more damage is done to the congregation when an open scandal goes unpunished. This is what is happening in our schools, where the children of our people are receiving this instruction. There is a division between our school and our Church. We do not celebrate the Christian festivals in the same way.

2. Damage is done to the congregation when our children are kept away from the services of the Church, especially the children's service. Damage is done to the congregation when its Word and Sacrament and Discipline are despised, when its pastor and elders are scoffed at.

Finally, damage is done to the congregation when signatures are sought from house to house of our members to support the sermon of a Thuringian preacher, a German Christian, who has been set up contrary to the laws of the Church and our Bible.

Truly, it is time to call for repentance and to exercise discipline when the whole congregation is in such danger, when damage is being done and the life of the congregation has become so worldly.

Whoever is offended by the church discipline, may he continue to be offended! It is a sign that he is not right with God or his Church. For the Church lives by the Word of God alone and is obedient to the Lord Jesus Christ alone. Church discipline does not seek to banish the sinner from the congregation, but to call him to repentance and to restore him. So teaches Calvin and so teaches the apostle Paul in his second letter to the Thessalonians: "Count him not as an enemy, but admonish him as a brother." '

This declaration was followed with a list of those called to repentance and forbidden the sacrament until they had shown sign of repentance. The battle between the pastor and the Party had started in earnest.

V

LAST DAYS OF FREEDOM

EVERY EVENING Paul was out and about on his motor-cycle. The Führer had made it clear that he intended to set in motion a church vote. This must be fought in every way possible and the people must be prepared for it, with suggestions for effective action. Thus Paul became involved in church politics, especially among the churches of the Confessing Church. He had invitations to about ten of the Hunsrueck villages to help them in this way. Of course, he aroused a good deal of hostility. Once he had a stone thrown at him, and I was always anxious when he was on one of these trips. It was the last evening before the voting that the accident happened. He was speaking in a German Christian parish and was due back later for a confirmation class at Womrath. That evening we waited—no Paul. I had to handle the choir by myself. It was the Friday before confirmation. Then came the news that Paul had had an accident in the fog. He was taken to hospital and, for a time, was very ill indeed. As it turned out, the accident had been a blessing in disguise. It delayed Paul's arrest and he was, therefore, still a free man when our sixth child was born on 13th May, 1937. It was a boy. We now had five boys and one girl.

Writing to my mother from hospital a week later, he said:

'It was a mercy that God dealt with me so gently on the night of my accident. The collision with the badly-lit lorry has only broken the gear lever of the cycle, and my leg. I must try to learn what lesson God is trying to teach me by laying me low at this time of festival in the life of the Church. I know you will call it a badly needed rest! Pray for me that I shall really learn his lesson. With a good conscience, I am enjoying myself here. I am undisturbed and can read and study. There are enough visitors to keep me from getting lonely. My shin-bone is broken in two places and the fibula in one.'

He thought much about church discipline during his time in hospital and hesitated before he issued his third proclamation of guilt. He felt that those who had not shown signs of repentance should be given as much time as possible to think the matter over. He was all for patience.

He was still in plaster of Paris over Whitsun, but nonetheless he insisted on taking three services. He went on preaching whenever he could and during his convalescence he hardly missed a Sunday. He had developed the method of writing his sermons out in full; but he gave them quite freely, in no way bound by the manuscript. He tended now more and more to preach from a text rather than to a theme. Over the winter of 1937 he had preached from the Gospels. The series had the overall title of 'The Glory of Jesus'. On 10th January, 1937, for example, he preached from Matt. 2.1-12; 'The Wise Men Visit the Child': 'A Call to Foreign Missions', 'A Call to Consolation and Thanks', 'A Call to Sacrifice and Service', 'A Call to show forth the Glory of Christ and His Kingdom'. The last sermon Paul preached in the regular ministry of his Church was on Luke 18.31-43. It was preached on Estomihi (Quinquagesima) 1937. Here is the full text:

'My dear people. We go again to-day through a new

gateway, entering into the holy Passiontide, where our
dear Lord and Saviour would take us unto himself and
say to us: "Behold we go up to Jerusalem." He waits
to see if we will take seriously, and truly mean, what
we have just sung: "Jesus, I my cross have taken, All
to leave and follow thee."

May he then take us to himself on this way to the
Passion, to suffering and to the holy cross? Or perhaps
we belong to those of whom it is said, "from that time
forward", i.e. from when he began to tell them of his
suffering and death, "many of the disciples followed not
after him". Our crucified Lord would take us with him,
up to the height of the cross, down to the depth of his
suffering, and, thereby, show us, gradually but clearly,
how deeply he loves us all.

It is of his great mercy that we may gather around his
cross on this approaching Passiontide. Our comfort and
our confidence are this, that, by his Word, he makes
known to us the way and prepares us for it. And now,
as we begin the journey at the very gate of the Passion,
he shows us so much glory and consolation, so much
light and grace, that we can almost see a signpost
pointing through the gate of the Passion, through
suffering to glory, through the cross to the throne!
This is the way of faith and by faith alone will it be
known.

When Jesus spoke to his disciples about his path
through suffering and death to the resurrection, through
shame and mocking and scourging to the rising again on
the third day, then the disciples could not understand.
They thought that that could not possibly be the way
of their dear Lord and Master, who lived so close to God
and who revealed God so clearly in signs and wonders
and healings. And although they knew that all must be
fulfilled in their Lord and Master, which the prophets
had said about the Son of Man, yet they did not under-

stand. It violated all their sense of reason. How could these disciples be expected to grasp the meaning of it? Given over into the hands of wicked men, shamefully used, killed, and could the matter yet come to a glorious conclusion? Because reason could not help the disciples to understand their Master's suffering and the cross, this Word and this Way of the Saviour through suffering to glory belongs to the realm of faith. By faith alone can this Word be understood. The Way of the Master is the Way of the disciple and his Church. That is what the apostles afterwards learnt and experienced. For the disciples and the Church also, the way to glory is through suffering and the way to the throne is through the cross.

That is why Jesus puts this among the blessings at the beginning of the sermon on the mount and all the other blessings have their power and meaning only insofar as they are taken together with this blessing. "Blessed are they which are persecuted for righteousness' sake", and "Blessed are ye when men shall revile you and persecute you and shall say all manner of evil against you falsely", and again, "Whosoever will come after me, let him deny himself and take up his cross." And yet, over it all, stands the promise that our faith shall conquer, that the world has been overcome, and that we shall live with Christ, reign with him, triumph with him, if here we have suffered with him and died with him. That is still as much against our feeling and our reason as the words of Jesus were for the disciples. The natural man sees the cross and the way of the cross only as the breaking of all human powers, the end and extinction beyond which there is no further way. Without faith, therefore, he can never be ready to go the way of the cross. Therefore, above all, his aim must be beyond human achievement to the glory of true victory. How stupidly men ask to-day, in various ways, about the

Church struggle: Isn't the Church almost quiet and in order again? Hasn't it nearly been settled? Yes, I think it has—so would the comfortable members of the Church like to think. They are already shocked at the struggle and suffering to which God has led us, and think it quite impossible for matters to go further. Insofar as they think that, they look round for every possible way out of this suffering and struggle. These are friends of the Church; but there are others, the enemies of the Church, who also seek to end the struggle. They reckon that our cause—the cause of Jesus Christ—is lost. They think they have only to get rid of a crowd of troublesome parsons and all will be quiet in the Church. Both of them, friends and enemies, are unable to see that, for the Evangelical Church, the way of death is the way of Jesus, the way of the cross, the way of life. A glance at Russia should teach us. There every outward form of organized Church life is destroyed, the pastors have disappeared and almost all the Church property is taken away. And yet there the Church of Jesus Christ lives more and perhaps grows stronger than it does here in Germany. It lives under the holy cross. Because of persecution, they gather together in one another's houses, where lay-preachers declare the Word of God and willingly take upon themselves the punishments of the law. Why then should not the way of the Church in Germany lead by way of far greater suffering and death, through total defeat, to victory and to glory? Don't be deceived: you can have no part in the glory of Jesus or his victory, unless you are ready to take upon yourself the holy cross and with him tread the way of suffering and death. For that, faith is needed, a faith which knows of the power and the victory of the cross. Such a faith is indeed a hidden and a quiet power, but not therefore ineffective or useless. No, it exercises itself in heartfelt prayer.

The blind man on the road to Jericho had heard of
Jesus, and that he was coming that day on his way to
Jerusalem. He believed on Jesus and waited for him. As
he passed by, he lifted up his voice and cried after him.
He paid no heed to those who tried to dissuade him or to
tell him that the Saviour was not there to satisfy his
need or to deal with his trouble. As he now stood before
Jesus, the firm and believing request came, "Lord, that I
may receive my sight." And Jesus sent him away with
the words, "Thy faith hath saved thee." The world is
blind to the way of Jesus and his disciples: the way
through suffering to glory. And we too are blind by
nature to his way. Our eyes are holden that we do not
see the hidden and the coming glory which shines
already on the way of suffering. We are like the blind
man, afraid, despondent, confused by our sorrow and
suffering, blind to the glory of the cross. We sit in the
midst of our ancient Christian culture like beggars
waiting by the roadside. We are no better than the
heathens who know nothing of Jesus. So are we blind
to the glory of the crucified Jesus, blind to the glory of
the way of the cross. We would far rather choose joy
and rapture than the disgrace of Jesus Christ. What
more do we need than to come with heartfelt prayer
and beseech our Lord to open the eyes of faith, that
we might see the glory of the cross. Then with this
glance of faith we shall be happy. We shall be contented
and rich, no longer sitting like beggars on the roadside
of the world, content to have a beggar's joy and a
beggar's pleasure. The world does not want to leave you
to Jesus or to let you follow in his way. It wants to
break the power of your will, right at the beginning of
the way of the Passion, that it might trap you in its
pleasures. It is the call of evil unbelief and not of faith,
when a man says, let us have one more fling with the
world's pleasure before Lent begins. That is no truly

inner choice, which stands shameless among the world's pleasures, intending to-morrow to become a follower of the cross. No. "Love not the world!" Carnivals and festivals have not grown out of the Christian faith and a true Christian will have nothing to do with them. Rather let us quietly assemble together and with due reverence prepare ourselves for the great feast. Let us come to our Lord Jesus and, full of faith, let us ask him that we might see the glory of his way to the cross. Rejoice that you suffer with Christ, for, if you suffer with him, you will also have joy and rapture at his appearing. Let us go out wearing his disgrace. So will he meet us as he met the blind man, and say to us: "Receive thy sight: thy faith hath saved thee."

And so, as followers of the cross of our Lord, we have a way given to us of God, a way through suffering to glory. And, in the long run, is it not the most beautiful and the best way through this earthly life? Is it not the only way by which we leave the beggarly life of this world and become truly the rich and blessed children of our rich heavenly father? Is this not the way by which we leave the husks of this world's meagre joy to feast at the banquet of our Lord's true pleasure? Even the disciples, who understood so little of the way their Lord had chosen, learnt to follow it faithfully and it led to pentecostal joy. The blind beggar who at one and the same time received the new light of sight and saw the glory of Jesus, also followed him and praised God. "And all the people when they saw it gave praise unto God." How else shall we enter through the gate of the Passion, how else shall we follow after Jesus than by giving praise to God? The Lord who goes before us to the cross, he will also strengthen us and keep us from evil. If we lose our life here for him, he will keep it unto everlasting life. He will let us see his glory here and there. Then through suffering we shall find our way to glory, through the cross to the throne. We shall believe that, according to his word, we shall trust his promise and, therefore, we shall give thanks to him with joy.'

VI

ARREST AND DISMISSAL

PAUL HAD his leg out of plaster on 28th May, but, of course, it still needed strengthening and massaging. He had little time to recover. I called him home for a particularly tragic funeral, which he held on 30th May in the church. On 31st May, he was arrested in his study by order of the Gestapo and taken to Coblenz for interrogation. We sat at home with no news until we heard through the Superintendent and later from the Administrative President that he was taken into protective custody in Coblenz. This caused a great stir in the town and no one was able to think of the reason for the arrest. Both our congregations sent four local farmers to Coblenz to the Gestapo. When they asked why their pastor had been arrested, they were told, (1) they could read it in the paper, (2) Pastor Schneider had stirred up the whole Hunsrueck area against the State, (3) their question was not proper, because they were not members of any organization. When they looked at the newspaper, they read, 'Protective Custody. Pastor Schneider of Dickenschied was arrested by the Gestapo, because he had spoken from his pulpit in an irresponsible way against a local farmer, urging the people to boycott him.' When they arrested Paul, the Gestapo gave him no time to pack. They said it was only for questioning. As soon as he arrived at the Gestapo headquarters in Coblenz, however, he was told: 'You'll be a long time in prison here', and at once taken to an underground cell. This cell was one of six or seven, which had formerly been strong rooms of the National Bank. Our friend, F.L., went to a great deal of trouble to see that Paul had all he needed. With great difficulty, he was able to arrange for Paul's washing to be passed on to him and, a little later, he managed to get his Bible through to him. With the first parcel of washing, I was able to smuggle a word of comfort to him. One day, Paul was led out of his cell. His photograph was taken from every angle and his fingerprints for the criminal records! It was all very harassing for him; but at this moment the porter, who was really the jailor, handed him another text that I had smuggled in. On it was written: 'Rejoice that your name is written in heaven'. That lit up his darkness for a while. At last the first message came through to us from him: 'Now, please, you my dear and all of you, please don't worry unnecessarily about me. All is in God's hands and he will use this matter for healing and not for destruction. Please don't try to move heaven and earth to get me free. You will only make life more difficult. Now we must bear our Christian obedience even against the powers that be, willingly suffering and trying to keep ourselves from all bitterness. We must wait with patience; our separation cannot be much longer. (3rd June, 1937.) His second letter was a greeting for the baptism of our child; but unfortunately it arrived a day late. It was a poem, such as he often wrote on days of rejoicing. It was written on June 10th and we had no further news. Why was there this delay in the post which amounted to a blockade? Paul had men around him, in the other cells, for whom he felt a deep concern. And they recognized this. Next door to him was an SS man, who had fallen from favour. He came from our area and admitted to Paul that he had often worked against him. Paul spoke with him as often as he could; but conversation between the prisoners was really for-

bidden. One evening, the SS man asked him about the
resurrection from the dead. He thought the air was
clear and so Paul spoke to him for about half-an-hour
on the Christian doctrine of the resurrection. In order
that he might hear everything, Paul spoke through his
window into a shaft connecting it with the SS man's
cell. Next day, Paul was questioned and reprimanded
for this breach. He was told that his letters would be
stopped. While the official was reprimanding and
threatening him, Paul took the opportunity to say that
he had been in prison quite a long time and that he
thought he ought soon to be told the reason for his
arrest. He was told that it had to do with his insistence
on church discipline, and was glad. Naturally, the
official would not take any responsibility for the charge
or discuss it.

Meanwhile, I had written to the Rhineland Council
about the arrest of my husband. All I heard was from
the Gestapo to say that, as a punishment, his letters had
been stopped. We were both without news.

Paul used all the paper that he could lay his hands on
to write a long letter to me, which he hoped to smuggle
out by a comrade who was leaving, but he arrived himself before the letter. Here are a few extracts from that
letter:

'I am content with the Word of God and the hymns.
For, apart from this, all I have to do is to clean out my
cell, make the bed and take about half-an-hour's walk
in the prison yard. So I have plenty of time to gather
together spiritual treasures for new service. Thus is my
time not fruitless. I hope it is also not fruitless for the
Church; that many want to overcome their spiritual
inertia and their avoidance of responsibility. So may
God send to us all a spirit of repentance and the desire
for a fully-disciplined church-life in the midst of this
godless generation. How much I have neglected and how

much better I must be prepared for the situation which is now coming upon us and which we have so long expected! We can reckon, I think, that I shall be kept here at least until the church vote is over. Meanwhile, my leg is not healing well and is obviously going to be shortened. The fibula is all right, but the shin bone has not knit. This imprisonment has not allowed it the proper treatment and I must reckon with being lame.

There are usually six or seven prisoners here of all sorts, but I seem to be the only pastor. Two young men, whose crime was that they were too friendly disposed towards the Pope, are now released again. You can imagine that life here has its own irritations and, above all, lacks purpose. To-day is now the sixth Sunday of my imprisonment and I have had no opportunity to take part in a service; but that does not mean I have not worshipped. I have already noticed that here, where all comfort is taken away, the soul becomes much hungrier and God's Word sinks much deeper into it. My fellow prisoner, the SS man, has given me half the flowers his wife sent to him. I have made a cross out of cardboard and given my cell a thorough Sunday-cleaning. So, in this clean cell, with the cross on a clean table, I held my service and felt strongly linked with my congregation at home. I have put your card with its challenge to rejoice under the flowers. You see, even here, we can have Sunday joy. I hope you have had it too. I hope you have gone for your usual Sunday walk and held your head high. Don't let them see you hanging your head. Let them see that we trust our God and can be patient in time of severe trial. Under the shadow of his wings shall always be our refuge. Let us see God's love in our suffering. This is not punishment or recompense for our sins, because Jesus has fully paid the price. No, this is the loving discipline of our Father, which we cannot refuse. If some, or even many brethren think they can

escape from suffering, simply because they want to
escape it, they may perhaps do so. But that will not
make them happier or more blessed. And so, my dearest,
don't be bitter against these brethren. They are the
losers. Our "suffering" is a step forward and soon we
shall see it as no suffering at all. Instead, we shall
"rejoice when we suffer with Christ". That is the only
way that we can see our suffering, as a "sacrifice,
acceptable unto God". Then we can bring it in the love
and in the spirit of Christ, that it might become a
blessing to the Church. This morning the Gospel reading
was of the seed growing secretly and it was a great comfort to me. So does the Confessing Church grow, not
depending upon our efforts to build it up or to extend
it.

Greet warmly my true friends in the churches and tell
them that I rejoice at the thought of coming again to
them. Now the storm has come; we have entered and
passed through it, "in nothing terrified" (Phil. 1.28-30).
Say also to my friends that it goes well with me and
that they must not worry about me, either now or in
the future. Rather let them be concerned that both we
and our children hold fast to the Word of God and the
witness of the gospel. Read the Epistle to the Philippians,
sing and pray.

God has softened the heart of the jailor towards us
and we are now doing well. To-day I had, for the first
time, a pint of fresh milk and I shall receive that now
every day. A fellow prisoner here daily massages my
leg and I hope it will soon be well. Brother Winterberg
has once again sent me a large food parcel with sausages,
cheese, tomatoes and other food. I fear that next time
he will send a trunk! The 23rd Psalm, which you told
me to remember, has come literally true. I do not want,
spiritually or physically. God cares for me truly and
most gently. He leadeth me daily into the green pastures

of his Word. As I long for you and for my people, he sustains my heart and gives me courage. His rod and his staff they comfort me.'

So he went on, quoting the Bible and giving me many passages to read for comfort and strength. He sent me also his prayer list.

On the morning of July 25th, I was standing before the door of our house, where a car waited to take me to one of Paul's close friends, when one of the young men from Womrath brought me a letter—a letter from Paul: 'I am in Womrath! Although banished from the Rhineland, I will preach there to-day. If you have the heart to do it, come over!'

I found Paul in the vestry. He looked ill and exhausted. The leg was bad. The friend in prison had helped, but he had not done enough. The leg needed far more regular care and better attention. I was worried. Sunday ran its course. All the church bells rang to let the people know that their pastor had come home. Until then, the bells had only been heard in times of mourning. In both churches, he preached from the text: 'If ye will not believe, ye shall not be established.' He said nothing openly about the banishment; but he asked the congregation to pray for him that he may remain with them. Many visitors and neighbouring ministers crowded in to the afternoon service. In the evening, we drove out to the manse of a friend and were then ready in the morning to consult a specialist about Paul's leg. It was that night that I learnt from Paul the details of his circumstances. The jailor had told him confidentially, 'To-morrow you will be banished; I have it on good authority from the office.' All that night, Paul was troubled. He wanted to be free; but he knew that this action—banning him from the Rhineland—was illegal. He must fight it. Earlier, he had maintained that the State had no right to banish a pastor from his parish,

C

unless he had broken the law. Now that he knew the
reason for his imprisonment, he was much more at rest.
He had a good conscience in refusing to obey the order
not to preach. He had not broken the law and was not
being punished as an 'evildoer'. On the next day, the
order to banish him was to be published and he entered
a protest against it. The banishment was based upon an
unjust and illegal arrest and imprisonment. He had been
appointed to his church by God and he could not now
betray his trust. His conscience was clear and his mind
determined. Despite his protests, he was put into a car
and driven to Wiesbaden, which was outside the Rhineland, set down and commanded not to return to his
parish. He walked straight to the station, threw the
banishment order into a rubbish bin and caught the next
train home. He stayed that night in a neighbouring town
and next day went to the house of one of his elders in
Womrath.

Our hope that a specialist might be able to put Paul's
leg right was soon disappointed. It would remain an
inch shortened. Paul gave the order, back home to
Dickenschied. I was worried as we went; but, on the
way, we met a friend called Langensiepen, who had
gone to much trouble to meet Paul. He argued with him
in a way that Paul understood and respected. Eventually,
he persuaded him to go to Baden-Baden for convalescence. Thus Paul went to safety. His first letter
from Baden-Baden was written on 27th July:

'Fritz will already have told you all that you need to
know about our journey and my settling in here. Pray
only that God will bless the way that I have taken. Perhaps it is not the way God had planned for me and I
do not clearly see his guidance; but pray that he may
bless it and use it for the establishing of our churches.
I hope it will not in any way bring shame upon our
people. There remains, however, to give thanks to God

for his gracious guidance during the past weeks. We must surely thank him for graciously leading me out of prison to my home and family and office. We can only be ashamed that we trusted God so little. He always does more than we can ask or think. Yet he must surely judge my lack of faith. And so, my dear wife, pray for me and help me to have greater faith. Let us both pray that we may take hold of the word: "Fear not, only believe."

The house here is very comfortable. Yesterday evening, before I turned in to sleep, I read again the letters you received during my time in prison. Surely we must be humbled by the many expressions of sympathy and loyalty, the many prayers, the tokens of concern, about which I had not the slightest idea when I was in Coblenz. We are in no way worthy of them, especially as we have not been as true in prayer and intercession as they have. We should have been praying for others, when we were thinking only of ourselves. These things call us to repentance. The judgment of God for these omissions has been somewhat kindlier than it seemed to be during the weeks of imprisonment. Do you know that it is the kindnesses of God which lead us to repentance? We shall know in future.'

And for the rest, the letter was personal. I did not go to him, because he thought it was safer that way and he gave me an address from which a letter could be forwarded. He wrote letters to others from Baden-Baden, which I have since seen. They all tell the same story of his rigid examination of his faith and trust in God. His keen sense of the importance of absolute honesty helped him through this period.

A week later I was able to go to Baden-Baden. It was a happy reunion; but I could see only darkness ahead. Paul stood in childlike trust, his struggles over: 'What is to be, will be. My Saviour in heaven knows what to

do with all that happens to me.' Then, I could ask him
the question I had longed to ask, ever since the night
he made his decision alone. 'Was it necessary for you
to forget your love for us on that night of decision?'
His reply lives with me: 'I have never loved you more
than on that night of decision. I wept for you.'

Then was I ready to accept his decision, to heed what
he had to say and to stand by him. Often, in those
weeks, it meant dying to one's own will, bending low in
obedience to God's will. I found it hard to do this,
especially when I saw the comparative quiet of the life
of many other pastors also belonging to the Confessing
Church. Why could Paul not be left alone too? He comforted me in my questionings: 'Don't you know that I
am one of the reconnoitring patrol, a scout sent out to
survey the land before the battle begins? Perhaps my
way is to be easier and my end better than those who
enter the turmoil of the battle!' Among all his visitors
in Baden, there was none he received more gladly than
Pastor Schlingensiepen. He came as a representative of
the Rhineland Council (of the Confessing Church). Paul
had sufficiently informed the Council about his treatment; but the president's representative came to learn
at first hand what he was feeling about it, how determined he was (and how determined I was, too) to continue in the way we had chosen. He left him free to
deal with his churches as he felt right, not with some
kind of ecclesiastical permission, but with respect for
Paul's obedience in the faith. They sealed their unity in
prayer. With understanding and emotion they bade each
other farewell and Pastor Schlingensiepen went on his
way, busily engaged in the work of the Confessing
Church. Paul was greatly encouraged. Pastor Schlingensiepen had invited him to attend a conference of all
those pastors who had been banished from their
parishes. He was obviously much concerned with the

problems involved and the meeting of the conference in the near future.

We remained on this semi-holiday in Baden-Baden for four weeks and left on 28th August—Paul's fortieth birthday. We celebrated; but a shadow lay over our festivities. The local Party official called to say that Paul must report within forty-eight hours to explain what he was doing. During the next months we were never together as a family again. He saw only the smallest of his children. The others had to be cared for by relatives. He and I and our youngest were like pilgrims with no settled life. When I spoke to him about our children, he always said that it was just because of them that we must be sure to be true to God. His lonely pilgrim way was not easy and often when he was among friends or old parishioners, they would ask with fear, 'But won't they send you to a concentration camp?' The shadow hung over him. Paul kept in close touch with the Rhineland Council. The proposed conference of banished pastors had not been possible, for a variety of reasons. During his last few days in Eschbach, he compiled a carefully-worded letter to the Government about his treatment and sent it to the Chancellor's office in Berlin, with a copy to the Rhineland Council.

Here is the letter:

PASTOR SCHNEIDER,
DICKENSCHIED (HUNSRUCK)

Eschbach, 30th September, 1937

To the German Chancellor at
  Wilhelmstrasse, Berlin.

Copies to the Minister of the Interior
  and the Principal Officer of State in Coblenz.

With all respect, allow me to submit to the highest offices of State, the following report:

I was arrested in my study on 30th May this year, shortly after my return from hospital where I had been treated for a broken leg-bone. The arrest was on the authority of the Gestapo. I was taken for interrogation to Coblenz and there put into prison. I was kept in prison without questioning and stayed there some time without trial. The reason given for my arrest, during my first few days in prison, was in some way connected with the statute of Hindenburg, February 1934, for the preservation of public safety and order. Apparently I was arrested for endangering the public safety. For nearly eight weeks I was held in prison without any opportunity to explain my actions, or any questioning or any trial. No effort was made to find if I had been justly or unjustly accused.

On 24th July, my banishment from the Rhineland was announced. Again the reason for the banishment had to do with the same statute. This time my behaviour apparently endangered the public safety of the whole province of the Rhineland.

I have already made myself clear to the Gestapo leader in Coblenz about the affair of the banishment. I have written to him saying: 'During eight weeks imprisonment no attempt was made to find out whether or not I had been justly arrested. The present announcement of my banishment is simply one more piece of evidence of the determined persecution of the Confessing Church, and thereby the Church of Jesus Christ in Germany. I must declare that the reason for my arrest based upon the Hindenburg statute is both untrue and unjust. I deny the validity of the order. Like my arrest, the banishment is also illegal. Hindenburg himself testifies against you when he says: "Take care therefore that Christ is preached in Germany." The Confessing Church does no more than that. I can neither recognize nor accept the banishment. I know that I have been called by God to my churches and cannot be separated from them by men. Not even the Government can wrench me away from them, unless it has been clearly shown that I have done wrong. I must therefore reject this order to take up my residence in some place outside the Rhineland. . . .

After making my position clear, I was forcibly taken by car out of the Rhineland. This action I deemed to be illegal for the reasons already given. I therefore returned to my church at once and, on the next day, preached in both my churches the Gospel of Jesus Christ. I preached that he alone is Lord and that we may not weaken in our confession of him. Since then I have been away from the Rhineland on a long holiday, which I needed because of my imprisonment and because my leg had not fully healed. This holiday alters nothing. I have taken my decision and will abide by it. I reject an unjust law of man and will disobey it. For this banishment of a pastor from his parish is a serious interference with the life of church and congregation. It is an attempt to put asunder the pastor and his people whom God hath joined together. 'Whom God hath joined together, let no man put asunder' is as true here as it is in the marriage ceremony. People and pastor are bound to fight against this unjust demand, even though it be made by those in authority. At the same time, it seems evident that such an illegal interference with the freedom and independence of the Church's life is contrary to the solemn guarantees given by the highest authorities of the German Reich. I will not be frightened by threats of punishments, whether they be threatened fines or arrests and new imprisonments. All these threats have been made in vain because God can deliver me from them if he will. He may deliver me by giving discernment to the authorities or in some other way. Even should punishment come upon me, I know this, that

God will avenge and justify all who suffer unjustly and that on his Judgment Day he will judge between me and my accuser. And as my accuser is 'the highest powers' or the 'powers that be', he will know how to distinguish a guilty obedience to Rom. 13.1. That was the text quoted to me at my banishment. As I rejected the banishment and declared my intention to disobey, I replied with the Acts 5.29: 'We ought to obey God rather than men.'

Now, I would like to mention a few points which, although they have in no way influenced the decision I have taken, might still affect the outward concerns of the Church.

The Christian instruction of young people in both my churches has been non-existent since March 20th, i.e. for half a year. For all this time the churches have been without regular pastoral care. Then, there is the further danger that, if this banishment is persisted in, the work will so deteriorate that no future pastor will be able to build it up again into a church. This has already happened in some smaller places and may happen to mine.

My six children look upon Dickenschied as their home, as I do. For I was born in the Hunsrück and, as a sign of my attachment to the parish, I have acquired there my own garden. My life is bound to Dickenschied. My treatment has been humiliating. I have been imprisoned and have endured harsh conditions. These things are not only unjust in themselves; they have disgraced my honour as a German citizen, as a man, as a Christian, as a protestant pastor, as a former German officer, and as one who fought 3½ years in the front line. I have been humiliated enough.

If I am further persecuted and if my churches are harder tried (for, make no mistake, they are devoted to their pastor and can see no guilt in him in this matter)

no right-minded man and especially no Christian will
be able to understand your action. Instead you will give
good grounds for a loss of confidence in the present
leaders of the State. . . .

Finally, I make one more comment, in which I hope
the voice of the Christian congregation may yet find the
ear of the authorities. Both my churches, through their
regular presbytery and in writing, have invited me to
return and continue to exercise my office. Thus, when
I refuse to accept this banishment, I am not relying only
upon my own conviction of what God would have me
do. My elders also, and my congregations, have taken
the difficult step of calling upon me to disobey the
orders of the authorities and themselves becoming
responsible for this disobedience. They dare to disobey
the authorities, because only so can they obey God who
is the Lord of the Church and the Lord also of the
authorities themselves.

Now then I commit my cause to the judgment of God,
from whom both the power of State and of Church is
derived. For to the one he has given the temporal sword
to punish evildoers and to protect the just; while to the
other he has given the spiritual sword, his holy and
eternal Word, until the Kingdom of God shall come in
perfect righteousness. Then, our Lord and Saviour, Jesus
Christ, will himself be both priest and king. Until that
day, we hold fast to his command : 'Render unto Caesar
the things that belong to Caesar and to God the things
that belong to God.'

On 1st October, we left Eschbach together. In Frankfurt we parted. Paul arrived that night at Kirn. From
here, I will let our dear friend Mettel take up the story :
'When I was a young man, I had the habit of staying
up half the night; but it once stood me in good stead. It
gave me a memory of Pastor Schneider which I shall

never forget. It happened one Friday night, or rather
Saturday morning, about half-past one. I was beginning
to consider going to bed when there was a loud knock-
ing on my window. I hurried to the door and there, to
my great joy, stood Pastor Schneider, holding out his
hand and saying, "Uncle Mettel, have you a place where
I can rest for a few hours?" He was, of course, more
than welcome and in no time I had coffee made and was
asking questions. "Where have you come from, and
where are you going?" He told me that he had been
home since his Coblenz imprisonment and that now,
despite his banishment from the Rhineland, he intended
to preach next Sunday in Womrath and Dickenschied. I
asked him if it were necessary to put himself into such
danger. Instead of answering me, he pulled out his Bible
and read with emphasis: "I am the good shepherd: the
good shepherd giveth his life for the sheep. But he that
is an hireling, and not the shepherd, whose own the
sheep are not, seeth the wolf coming, and leaveth the
sheep and fleeth: and the wolf catcheth them, and
scattereth the sheep. The hireling fleeth because he is
an hireling, and careth not for the sheep. I am the good
shepherd." Each time he read, "I am the good shepherd", he did so with deliberate emphasis and with his
finger raised. He had identified himself with his Lord in
this rôle. After a long silence, which was itself full of
meaning for both of us, I said, "Go forth, then, in his
name". And we prayed together before we went to
rest.'

Next day, Paul came home, and how glad we were to
have him! Yet we knew the danger he was in. How
much I wanted to hide him and make him rest until
he was truly well! His mind, however, was not on rest,
but on the harvest festival. A quick bath, a good sleep
and then a hilarious morning with the children. The
morning was quiet, because the first service was not

until midday. The greater part of the congregation were overjoyed to see their own pastor back in his rightful place again. A young colleague in the Confessing Church gave the blessing and Paul preached from Psalm 145.15-21. He urged that all Christ's people should praise the Lord, openly and not in a corner. It was an appeal to the Confessing Church to confess her Lord before men, before the world, despite the danger of the time. 'That,' he said, 'shall be our harvest thanks.'

We sang and all seemed as it had been before; but anyone whose eyes were clear could see what dangers hung over the pastor. After the blessing, he stood awhile in his pulpit with pain and love for his people. In the afternoon, we had all the elders in for coffee. A few hours of quiet and happiness together. Paul prayed with the children before he left for Womrath to conduct the evening service there. We went by car. Already, a long way off, we could see their lights blinking: somehow, I knew at once that it was the police. The arrest did not take long, but at least Paul had time to stick a Bible and a hymnbook into his pocket. The police in Dickenschied had also been looking for him. He was placed temporarily in the prison of the neighbouring town of Kirchberg. Next day I was in his jailor's kitchen, when I heard him singing. He had heard my voice and sung as loud as he could, 'A Safe Stronghold our God is Still'. While I stood on the steps and he at the door of his cell, we were able to speak to each other. 'Tell the Church,' he said, 'that I am and remain the pastor of Dickenschied and Womrath.'

He was always resourceful and, as I left, I could see that he had found the one place in the little window where he could wave good-bye. Then he settled down to write letters—to the children, to his elders and to his nearest friends. In the afternoon, four women from the Womrath church made their way to Kirchberg to see

their pastor. Of course, they did not get permission to
see him; but the jailor's wife showed them a woodshed
where they could hear and talk to their pastor through
the very window from which he had waved good-bye.
Paul pushed out to them a scrap of paper and they
brought it back in triumph. 'Many, many thanks, my
dear women! We are already a little nearer. God will
one day fully accomplish what he has begun. I am and
remain your pastor. Pray God will turn all that happens
into good and a blessing to our church. Your visit has
strengthened me and given me great joy. Rejoice in the
Lord always. We have no need to rage against evil and
angry men. They have their Judge. They will not be
allowed to destroy the Lord's people. God will again
bring us together.' It was signed 'your true pastor
Schneider'.

The next day he was taken to Coblenz, spent a short
period in the Gestapo building and was then placed in
a cell at the police station. It was a small, primitive cell,
only four feet by fifteen feet. His treatment was quite
normal. He was allowed to have food brought to him.

Meanwhile, the elders at Dickenschied and Womrath
stood firmly behind him and wrote to the Minister of
the Interior at Berlin. They complained about the treatment of their pastor, sent copies of letters they had
received and asked for him to be restored to them. It
was a brave letter and they did not hesitate to add their
signatures. Paul also sent his protest. But all to no effect.

He came to distrust the arrangement for sending
letters home and developed his own unofficial system.
He put his letters, carefully hidden, inside his laundry.
Only the police inspected this, not the Gestapo. These
were his 'unofficial letters' and are so marked in the
following chapters. His advice to me was 'Seek and ye
shall find.' He drew pictures of himself for the children
and composed little rhymes, whose humour showed him

to be in good spirits—'Father's view from the verandah —a chestnut tree', 'Father sitting on the verandah', 'Undisturbed study', and so on. The 'verandah' was a bench placed up against one wall and so arranged by Paul to give him a view from the window, with the other wall as a footrest!

Once I was able to see him and talk with him for three-quarters of an hour.

VII

LETTERS FROM PRISON

WOMRATH WOULD have to look after itself yesterday. The police did not wait long. Many thanks for the pyjamas. I am afraid now you have all your troubles over again. Give my greetings to our people next Sunday. I hope that Womrath did manage to hold their service yesterday after all, for I suppose God expected that of them. I was sorry that I could not get through. If we had arranged everything in complete trust, then God would have delayed the police a quarter of an hour or perhaps saved us the necessary quarter-hour delay. So, let us take from God, as good, whatever comes. Perhaps my responsibility for the church can be dispensed with. Gather together in homes and in the church with prayer and God's Word. Pray for the powers that be and for the church. Now are we all again enrolled in his army: he cares for all whom he loves. How quickly this consolation comes to us again! I am very glad, however, that I was able to get to Dickenschied, because there the need was greater. Next time it will be Womrath's turn. I hope it will be soon.

Now, let us hold fast to our faith and trust in the power of God to work miracles still. The churches must not let themselves be frightened. We stand alone and there is, therefore, all the more reason to throw ourselves upon God. We must pray more faithfully.

KIRCHBERG, 4th October

Dear children! It was lovely that father could be home on Sunday once again and even look in to the church! I was happy to see you all together and not quarrelling. Unless you are like that, agreeing one with the other, God cannot hear you when you pray for father. Go on being friendly, even more than ever. I know that God hears you and your little prayers are built together into a strong wall that surrounds and protects us. So, even your father cannot be harmed. Not a hair of his head will be hurt unless it is God's will. Please go on praying. Pray that God in his power and grace will bring father back to Dickenschied and that we all may live and remain in Dickenschied. While we are waiting for God to answer our prayer, don't be naughty or think that God does not hear us. And don't get tired because God seems to take a long time. He may have his reasons. 'God helps us when we need him.' Remember that. Although I am not able to come home, I am not really very far from you here in Kirchberg. Perhaps God will move the hearts of the men in the Government to let father go free. If not, we must think that he has a reason. Perhaps these men need to hear more about God's Word and his dear Son, who is our Saviour, and perhaps they have yet to learn to believe. I am glad that you are with your dear mother, all safe and happy. Be kind to your mother and love her. Every day learn a little more writing and reading and arithmetic. Learn every day a little verse and a wise saying. Your father loves you.

COBLENZ, 10th October (Unofficial)

For a week now, my dear, I have been away from you, on service in the holy war of the Church of Jesus Christ. What is going to happen to me I do not yet

know. Possibly the Concentration Camp. Within a
reasonable time, it will be decided. Then we shall be
able to adjust ourselves to it and the time of uncertainty
will be over. In any case, I am still in no doubt that my
decision and my actions were right. I do not regret
them. Perhaps you too, my dear, are now sure in your
heart that we have taken the right way. Perhaps now
the happenings in the Church and the news of similar
happenings among the brethren has convinced you that
we were right not to yield to the demands of the Government in this matter. Above all, God will continue to
stand by his promises, sustaining us and helping us by
his almighty power. He will comfort us and bless us in
all our sufferings. Whoever wishes to avoid suffering
now must be careful lest he be rejected by God. I simply
cannot understand how or why God gives freedom to
men to choose whether they will join in active resistance
to the State or whether they will make intercession for
the brethren who are witnessing to their faith in suffering. Therefore, take courage even if we must continue to
be the only ones to go into the depths of persecution.
'Think it not strange concerning the fiery trial which is
to try you, as though some strange thing happened unto
you: but rejoice inasmuch as ye are partakers of
Christ's sufferings.' He comes quickly and, in the last
days, there will be times of refreshing before the face
of our God. Then all your grief and sorrow shall be
turned into joy and laughter.

COBLENZ, 17th October (Unofficial)

Your dear letter of the Saturday before last reached
me yesterday, i.e. Saturday, and it could not have come
at a better time. It helped me to keep the Lord's Day
with rejoicing. How much this piece of paper can mean
to me, telling me that you are still there! Especially the

end of your letter comforted me and strengthened me. Now, we may live through this experience together and suffer together. God is training and trying our faith in him and our love of him. We know how much we need this, because we were poor beginners.

I am so sorry that you have not yet heard from me. I know that my condition always seems worse to you and to the others than it really is. I don't want you to think that. I wrote to you the Monday before last, but that letter has just been returned, as your letter to me arrived. I must begin again and tell you all the news in this letter, which should get through to you. You will know already that I was taken on the evening of 4th October to the well-known building in 'Vogelsang' in Coblenz. It was a very quick journey despite some stops on the way. For the first four days, I was in my old cell again, cell 1. I was examined there twice. All these days I have been very sad and lonely. I have wondered how things were going with you and I have felt deeply the sorrow of our parting, the sorrow of separation from you and from the church. I have felt myself far from home. I must admit that it was a great comfort to me one day to hear another bird singing his lovely song outside my window. Apart from him, I have had no company.

On Friday, 8th October, I was brought to my present abode, a few streets away from 'Vogelsang' ['bird song']. On the whole, it is more comfortable and deserves far more the name of Vogelsang than the other did! For here, my little window looks out, albeit through blinkers of sheet iron, on the top of a chestnut tree. In this tree, I can see the sparrows playing or a little tomtit or a pair of thrushes. This time, I am not underground, but on the second floor, although the view is somewhat spoiled by the sheet-iron blinkers. The cell is about three and a half feet wide, fifteen feet long ten

feet high. The air is much drier and healthier. The
window lets in more fresh air than in my old cell. The
cell is also much better heated. My furniture is very
simple. I have no table and must balance my basin or
my plate on my knee. I am writing this letter, partly on
the window-seat—the only seat in the cell apart from
the bed, which also makes a wonderful seat—and partly
on my knee. The cell is lit by an electric light, hidden
somewhere above my cell: concealed lighting! Now for
the bed, which I have already mentioned as a wonderful
seat and which I have enjoyed since yesterday. It has
an iron frame, without springs or any other such luxury;
but it has a very pleasant mattress made of real seaweed.
This in a way makes up for the absence of a table. These
two, bed and seat, together with the width of my cell,
determine my way of life. A very much better way of
life than I have had until yesterday! The other cell was
much darker and was furnished only with a plank bed.
Over the mattress, we have a white sheet and a blue-
checked cover, which can be stuffed to keep us warm.
For all this luxurious provision, I was glad to have the
white cloth you sent me. Please send a fresh one each
time with the washing. We have enough food and it is
well cooked. Our meals are cooked by an older woman,
who also serves it (at least, she fills up our basin or
plate, or mug and whatever we hold out to her in the
corridor!). In the morning, we have coffee with bread
and marmalade; at midday, a thick soup and perhaps
some mashed vegetables, with an occasional piece of
sausage or meat; in the evening, porridge or oatmeal
soup of bread and cheese with coffee or rice. To-day,
being Sunday, we had for our midday meal a mixture
of potatoes and carrots with sausage, and for our
evening meal, cocoa with bread and butter—or rather,
margarine. It is also possible to buy extra for yourself.
You have to have all your wits about you both to get

your morning wash and to buy these extras. However, it can be done when you know how. Unfortunately, I have had very little opportunity to know my fellow prisoners. I hardly ever see them. All I know is that there are 7-10 of them and they are a mixed bunch. Occasionally—it was the fourth time yesterday—I am allowed out in the fresh air for about half an hour. It is an event and I make the best of it with vigorous exercise.

There now, you are fully informed about my outward condition. I have written in great details so that you can imagine my life here. So long as I am here you must not worry yourself too much about the hardships of my prison. Don't be too disappointed that they won't allow you to visit me. We shall so think of each other that we shall be truly close to one another, even when separated like this. This time I have my Bible and my hymnbook. They have both been a great help to me; but I need more to keep my mind working and my thought clear. I want to collect some books around me and plan out my reading. Could you send me the collection of Lutheran and Reformed Confessions, the Heidelberg Catechism and a few numbers of the *Evangelische Theologie*.

My dear wife, I often sit and think what an unnatural father I am and why I have brought all this upon you and whether I have the right to do so. Then I begin to sit in true repentance in my cell—and it's a very suitable place for that! But we can do no other. This is the way God has led us. I have thought and thought, but I cannot yet see how we can avoid going in this way. So, with complete trust, we must leave our affairs in God's hands and let him justify us. By faith are we justified in all our sin, but he will also justify us before the world in his own good time. My dearest, I am so thankful to God for his kindness in allowing me to have those wonderful

weeks with you and the children. Now, we will trust
the promise of the Lord that he who leaves all he has
and all his own, for the sake of Jesus, will receive back
a hundredfold in this world and, in the world to come,
live everlasting. The chestnut tree becomes for me God's
greater and more beautiful world. This world becomes
for me the even lovelier world of God's eternity. 'As
having nothing, and yet possessing all things.' The Lord
Jesus grant me a persistent sense of this possession until
I come to him.

COBLENZ, 18th October (Unofficial)

After I had written to you yesterday an official letter
as my special Sunday privilege, I decided to write to-day
an unofficial one. God knows if and when it will gladden
you. I am sitting on my favourite window-seat, looking
at the chestnut tree. It is quite yellow now and winter's
dead hand is trying to snatch the leaves from the tree,
but they are still holding fast with all their ebbing
strength. Already the fine shape of the tree is emerging,
which soon will give dignity to the naked and cold
branches. So the autumn and the winter storms come
over the Church and Christianity and it will be shown
what was only leaves and what solid, a true part of the
tree. In this world truly it will come to pass even as in
the parable of Jesus. Life will come out of so naked and
cold a thing as a tree in winter. Let us not be troubled
by the sad and sorry appearance of the Church, which
for those who can see has also its beauty.

Now, a word or two about my fellow-prisoners.
There is a Czech here who is giving me a correspondence
course in English, in return for some help that I am
giving him. He was a locksmith once, but has recently
been a tramp. He writes a good hand and has carefully
prepared two pages of English words, with pronuncia-

tion and a few sentences for a beginner to practise. He has also confided to me a beautiful prayer, giving thanks to God the Father, which he has written himself. He is an intelligent man. Then, there is the earnest Jehovah's Witness woman. I have been brought two cells nearer to her and am now separated from her by only one small cell. Last Sunday, we were able to have an exchange of notes through the cell door. I am sorry for the poor woman with her tense nerves. She has already been a long time in prison. The Mr O., whom you know, has examined her and is working on her case. And then there is an Italian and a Pole, both good fellows in their own way; but when they go out for a walk in the court- yard, they spend all their time looking for cigarette ends, which they can later make up into new cigarettes to smoke! So they are always looking downwards and lose half the fresh air they could breathe. There ought to be a moral in that somewhere. When a man is the slave of his passions, so he goes searching for bits and pieces to satisfy him. . . .

In my cell, night is already falling and only here at the window is it possible to see at all. Before it gets too dark, I must write out an evening prayer for my Czech friend and his companions in the hope that I can smuggle it to them this evening.

May God bless the coming of the new pastor to take up his work. The people should receive him with thanks and love. Give him all that he needs and help him in every way you can.

May God's blessing keep us close and fold us in his love.

COBLENZ, 24th October, 1937 (Unofficial)

The cook and cleaner seem to wish me well and, so far, even the police have not been unpleasant. Once this

week I was moved to a much better cell. It was larger
and much lighter. But in the middle of the night it was
needed to take three beds and house three women
prisoners. I was shifted back to my old cell. In that mid-
night shift, I found the police very helpful. Apparently,
some of the staff here had suggested my move to a better
cell. A kindness which deserved better results. On Tuesday, I was taken downstairs for questioning on the basis
of information given by . . . and Frau . . . It concerned pastoral visits I made last autumn. This was the
first I had heard about these two complaints. I was
shocked to discover how perfectly innocent pastoral
work can be twisted to sound like a political denuncia-
tion. Of course, I was able to explain and, if it comes to
a proper trial, I hope that I shall know how to account
for my words. With God's help, I will. I suppose this
preliminary enquiry was to decide whether my case was
ready for trial. I could almost wish that the final trial
were over and I had an end to this suspense. I want to
explain my case whether it comes out all right or not.
The enemies of the gospel will in the end hang themselves with their own rope. Our task is simply to forgive
them as we are taught in the gospel for we too are
unfaithful servants. The questioning on Tuesday was
largely routine and not very intensive. Every day this
week, except one, we have been allowed to take our
walk in the courtyard. At first, most of us walked about
as we pleased, quite unorganized. I went my own way
at my own fast pace. The Czech and now the two other
young fellows have attached themselves gradually to
me, while the older prisoners, the Jehovah's Witness
and the Pole went their own quiet way. Yesterday I
again walked by myself because the others were
dragging behind. They seemed tired. I was not, and
wanted the strenuous exercise of a quick walk. You
see how much stronger I am getting, and my leg is ready

for service. . . . Now I am back in my penitence cell,
which has already become dear and friendly to me. It is
astonishing how a place which in itself is wretched can
take on so homely an air. The properly made bed, the
bench and the wall seat, the plain window newly
cleaned, with its view of the chestnut tree, have an air
of comfort. This is heightened now that I have fixed
your picture on to the inside of the door and Martin
Niemöller's on the wall. I have fastened these two pictures with a sticky paste I acquired yesterday. And so,
when I sit at my balcony seat, by the open window, as
I am now sitting to write this letter, or simply to admire
the golden sun of the autumn afternoon transforming
the chestnut tree, then I seem truly to be enjoying life
and envy no man in the world. . . . Now that I know
our church has an assistant to care for it, I can enjoy
the quiet of this place the better. It is good that our
churches' trust in the Confessing Church has been
rewarded in this way; but remind the people that he is
not paid by the State. He is our man and he can only
stay among us if we stand by him to the point of sacrifice. . . . Again this morning I had my own service,
with Gospel and Epistle, Prayers and Hymns. That is
when I especially remember all of you at home. The
Scriptures told me again of the glorious freedom of the
children of God. After service, I read and did some
English study. After an afternoon nap, I went back to
my window seat and here I am still. It is already seven
o'clock and soon my evening meal, with cocoa and
bread and margarine, will be coming in. At a quarter to
eight, the lights will go out, so that the jailor can go
home. I shall then begin to repeat what I have been
learning during the week. All this week I have read and
learnt passages from Isaiah and Romans. Time does not
hang on my hands.

COBLENZ, 31st October, 1937

Once again it is Sunday afternoon, already the third
Sunday of my imprisonment. Even in prison, God has
shown his promise to be true that on the Sabbath day,
which he has ordained, he will come with rich blessing.
Out of his word and with festive joy he has brought
peace to my cell and to my heart. I believe our other
prisoners have felt so too. After our midday meal, we
had our walk in the courtyard. I was glad that this time
we were all together and marched in order—Pole,
Italian, Czech and Pastor. I had to restrain myself to a
moderate pace, but did so gladly. This has not been the
rule during the week. Each has been left to go at his
own rate. This former disorderly walking was part of
an order to keep us from talking to each other. On
special occasions and whenever the opportunity was
given, I did speak some serious words to them. The
Czech has often approached me and I feel a concern
for him. One of his approaches earned him a punishment and we were all in danger of losing our Sunday
letter and our weekly visit. This morning, we are all
back in favour again and the threat of punishment is
gone. The papers which you brought have come to us
in our cells and they are like a true Sabbath blessing.
The young Italian has read them most closely and under-
stands why I am imprisoned; the earnest Jehovah's
Witness approves most heartily of the Geyser sermon;
the aged, thoughtful Pole, who has a lovely character, is
asking for more papers on these lines; the Czech, when
he has overcome his pride and his resistance, will change
his unbelieving attitude. I am not sure how much the
young Pole means by his profuse thanks, but I entrust
him to God and believe that some good will come out
of this time for him. These men have now been my
companions for three weeks and you see that I have

already a small church and pastoral responsibilities. Our good cook has had an accident and broken both bones in her arm. I was able to send her a greeting in the hospital and also put some papers in with it. You see what a wonderful service you have done with those leaflets. Your visit on Friday was a great joy, throwing a flood of light into my life and giving me a happy memory to hold in my mind. Please give my true thanks to Brother Petry for bringing you here and for what he has done since. Perhaps we shall still need to use the hard words of the letter to the Corinthians. Now, are we both thankful to God that He has, with the help of the assistant, so cared for our church and our home. We must learn to be thankful that he has given to me so peaceful a sanctuary, wherein his blessings are evident. We must not deceive ourselves, lest later we become disappointed. My situation is very serious and we must face it. Things are not getting better. After your visit on Friday evening, I met Herr O., whom you have met already. He urged me to sign a document saying that I accepted my banishment and would not again attempt to return to the Rhineland. Naturally, I refused, explaining the nature of my call and the bands which bind a shepherd to his flock. He countered by saying: 'Can't you see that you are heading straight for the Concentration Camp?' I said that I couldn't see where I was going, but if I must suffer that then I would suffer it. Clearly my case, despite last week's interrogation, is not yet ready for trial. Herr O.'s threats may well have been the usual attempt at intimidation, but I suspect this was also the answer to my letters to the authorities. Whatever be the meaning, Herr O. said to me before he left that, in the next few days, I can expect my case to go further. After the first shock of this blunt statement, I began to realize what it meant. I am satisfied that he was speaking he truth, that his threat was not idle

and that I must be prepared for the Concentration Camp.
I am content. I know that God, who has dealt so kindly
with us until now, will continue to be by our side and
will allow no circumstance to be harder than we can
bear. Herr O. also gave me your letter of the previous
day—the quickest that any of your letters has come. So
I had a double visit from you on the same day. The
letter was just what I needed after the first shock,
reminding me, as you so sweetly did, that God had
commanded us not to fear, but to be of good courage.
Like your letter of a week ago, it was one more example
of the little kindnesses of God.

The chestnut tree is now almost bare. The last few
days have robbed it of its last leaves. But the sky is blue
and clear in these last days of autumn. The birds tumble
over themselves with joy in the cool sunshine and are
still quite merry on its bare branches. This is a parable
perhaps of our home life, which has been hard and bare
this past year. Until this came upon us, everything in
our family life had been so good and beautiful. Now the
beloved cross has been set up there also; but that too
will most certainly show us that God is true. He will let
his eternity, the Kingdom of Heaven, shine even more
brightly through the troubles than it shone through the
joy. Our little children, the dear merry birds, will sing
happily on the branches of our faith, our love, our hope
and our prayers.

And so, if there is to be at this time no return—and
it is not at all clear that such a return in any case would
not lead to a new struggle and a new turmoil—we shall
not grow weary. Our longing for a time of quickening
in our family life, for time together, for harmony, for
peace, must not weary us. An imprisonment can last a
long time and we must prepare ourselves for that. In
different forms, the Jehovah's Witnesses have already
suffered much in camps and prisons. We pastors must

be ready to face as much. In many cases, the wives of the Jehovah's Witnesses are also in prison. We must be thankful that you are at home and able to look after our little ones. It isn't really so bad for us men.

Now I must battle with the writing pad, in which you have so cleverly pasted your notes to me between the pages of the block. My writing is now holding a regular conversation with yours between the lines! All is now well. What you tell me about the state of affairs in our congregation and in the Church generally only confirms my view about the importance of my own case. I am more than ever convinced now that my refusal to accept a banishment from the State, which was ordered without legal grounds, and which is now to be enforced by the threat of punishment and imprisonment, is of paramount importance for the relation of Church to State. It concerns the freedom of the Church to preach the gospel in season and out of season. I understand less and less the attitude that we must confine ourselves to wordy resolutions as long as we are allowed to operate as legally recognized bodies. I hope the Church leaders, who so far have said little about my case, will recognize the importance of the issues involved and find the words to express their principles. Or do I have to remain the one little pastor of the whole Hunsrück area who has to show the State what is right? Is it not asking too much of the State that it should take a serious decision, which ought to be taken boldly by the Church? Why have the church leaders been silent for three months, since I refused to accept my banishment? I wrote to them quite clearly, pointing out that I considered this decision to be their concern. They should have directed me one way or the other. It seems to me that the future of the Church in Germany depends not upon its leaders, but upon the separate congregations, the local churches and their pastors. We can do without our clever church politicians unless they are prepared to fight their battles in their local church and from the base of a single congregation. From now on, I see my struggle as a struggle for an indissoluble link—at least, indissoluble so far as man is concerned—between pastor and people. This alone is right and it is also necessary for the continued life of the Church. . . .

The way in which our children are forced to use the so called 'German greeting' [Heil Hitler!] has often worried me. I can understand that they do it without thinking, because they are ordered officially so to do, at the beginning and the end of every conversation. Don't let them continue in it without thinking; tell them that father considers it to be idolatry. Refer them to Acts 4.12.

COBLENZ, 7th November, 1937 (Unofficial)

I understand that the authorities are greatly embarrassed by us protestant pastors. They are afraid to torment us any more because it is not at all clear to them what they will achieve with their further punishment and they have no wish to make 'martyrs' of us in the cause of the Church to which we unmistakably belong. Yet, even if they let us alone, that too is a triumph for the gospel and the embarrassment remains. The question has still to be honestly answered: Why did they imprison us?

Pray God that common sense will prevail, even the common sense of the church politicians, so that our people may be spared the worst consequences of the mad philosophy of Rosenberg and the church reformers. But, as God will! If it must be pushed through to its logical and fanatical consequences and we must reap the harvest we have sown, then in God's name let it be as quick as possible. . . . Now that all my aches and

pains are over, I am sitting with pleasure at my balcony,
writing, in the morning. I have made some progress
with the Catechism, Isaiah and Romans, but have not
been working so intensely as I wanted to because of my
cold earlier in the week. On your last visit, you asked
me what I did all day long. Principally I have become a
pupil in the school of God's Word and I want to remain
that way. I can make up for some of the time I wasted
when I was studying. This imprisonment gives me an
opportunity to learn the things I missed or neglected.
So, to-morrow morning I shall work at the Bible,
to-morrow afternoon at the Confessional documents,
reading, writing and committing to memory. These two
pages for the children will let you all know how I work.
The day and even the week is so carefully apportioned
that the time does not seem long, but rather the
opposite. This morning my coffee with bread and honey
tasted particularly good. The little piece of news you
slipped in, that another pastor had refused to accept his
banishment and was in prison, rejoiced me. Of course I
feel for the poor brother and know what he is suffering;
but I am glad that another pastor has taken the same
step. It is a kind of justification of my own conscience,
of my own action. Now, I wait only for our church
leaders to speak out clearly on this question of banishment, not so feebly and ambiguously as in Augsburg.
This morning, I began my service with a verse from
Psalm 33. I rejoiced to read in the gospel of the power
that makes the dead to live (the request of Jairus to
Jesus), of the act of Jesus which truly made sport of
death (the maiden is not dead but sleepeth), of the faith
of the woman with the issue of blood who pressed in to
touch the hem of his garment, seeking health and finding
it. The Epistle made me want to pray for all those things
the Apostle lists for us: 'wisdom and spiritual understanding', especially that we might understand the

Scriptures and the power of God; 'walking worthy of the Lord unto all pleasing, being fruitful in every good work', so that we give the enemy no ground whereby he may bring our faith to shame; 'knowledge of God', truly now like a mirror to a dark world, the ground of all knowledge in which we have eternal life; 'strengthened with all might, according to his glorious power, unto all patience and long-suffering with joyfulness'. It is to our shame that we still need to be admonished by the Apostle in the same words; but a great joy to know that all these things are available and we may even now begin, weakly perhaps, to enter into them. Let us praise God for his kindness. Yes, 'Blessed be the God and Father of our Lord Jesus Christ, which according to his abundant mercy hath begotten us again into a lively hope by the resurrection of Jesus Christ from the dead, to an inheritance incorruptible and undefiled, and that fadeth not away, reserved in heaven for you' (I Pet. 1.3-4).

Should not that hope be enough to carry us through this earthly life? Should not that hope be enough for all who will receive it to give them power to live and grow, enough for all except those who in unbelief and hardness of heart refuse to accept it? Should not God be able to renew his Church, which he has rescued out of this world, with that hope, renew it even in this dangerous time? The chestnut tree preaches to me again and spreads out to me its dark, bare branches, holding its little dark buds, full of hope for next year. I can see the buds quite near to the window, and high up on the topmost branch. They were already there before the golden leaves which wrapped them round had fallen from the tree. Perhaps we have not noticed the growing bud, hidden under the leaves of a withering Church, because of our thanklessness and our little faith. . . . The Confessing Church when it is true to itself is a tree with buds; the hidden congregations within the congregations are the buds of the Church. There, if you look, you can see the buds, where men are prepared to go as pastors where no pastor is recognized. There are the buds, where men refuse to take a secure position guaranteed by the State, because such positions are no longer positions of honour and faith. There you can see the buds amidst all the vagaries and double dealings of church politicians; there you can see already with the spiritual eye the coming Church and its spring. Certainly the world and the unspiritual churchman see the bare tree of its culture, of its outward form robbed and condemned, so that it seems almost finished, fit only to be used for firewood, like the idols. This is what the Church appears like to such when it is deprived of the recognition of the world and of the State. For they have put their trust in a false church, a State religion which has grown up around them and which they now very rightly see to be a condemned tree. Their pride becomes fit for ashes. As the prophet said: 'They feed on ashes.' But we sit quietly in the branches of a poor, bare and humbled tree. They can see no hope in it. To us, it stretches out its buds in promise. These buds of the apparently dead tree, and these alone, carry the promise that 'the gates of hell shall not prevail against them'. Only here can we dwell safely. Only in faith, which is the indestructible power of its life and its buds, is there true freedom and true joy. And we shall continue to hold fast to this faith, because in it alone is 'the victory which overcometh the world', which overcomes prison and death. Let the world keep its rewards and promises. I would rather have my faith. One day the buds will burst, the cross will reveal the crown.

COBLENZ, 14th November, 1937 (Unofficial)

At my window on Tuesday I witnessed one of those pagan ceremonies which abound to-day. It was a celebration of the 9th November performed by the special police. You know the kind of thing: 'Not in sorrow and grief, but in pride do we remember the sixteen who gloriously died', and so on. The usual glorification of those men. 'We live and struggle for Germany, a Germany which endures through all eternity. We ask for a total sacrifice, of body and soul, a total commitment of our thought.'

Apart from that spectacle, life has been peaceful during the past week. I really believe that I am now greatly profiting from my regular Bible reading and have progressed in my understanding of the Holy Scriptures. How unbelievably deep is the Wisdom of God and how shallow beside it is the wisdom of this world with its lies and sins! The foolishness of God is wiser than men. My other reading is not going so well. I am still stuck in the historical introduction to the Confessional Writings and the Czech is not at all satisfied with my progress in English!

Herr O. came to-day and asked me about my sermon notes, which are apparently needed by the prosecution for my trial. When I refused him and said that they would be quite unintelligible, he said that he would have my house searched from top to bottom. I must take my stand on this. I cannot hold myself responsible to any man for the way in which I prepare my sermons. These notes are personal and private. My sermons and my notes are two quite different things. I am never bound to my notes. Sometimes what I say is sharper and sometimes much milder than what I have noted down. These notes are simply helps to me. The sermons have been freely preached, and anyone could have come in to hear them. If they want to find grounds for my imprisonment or my banishment, they must find it among witnesses who heard me preach and not among notes I used to prepare my sermons. My attitude to the State must not be deduced from these notes, proving that I held one view rather than another of the function of the State. But of this also I am quite sure: I am not responsible to the State for what I preach. We are responsible to the Lord and to his Church. It is the Lord we serve. If now, despite my refusal, my notes are searched for, found and seized, don't be too worried about it. I shall be able to account for what I said and stand by it. In our sermons, none of us has ever said too much; we have all said far too little. I don't think that I need get unduly worried on that account. One thing, however, is clear now: we must not expect my case to be settled soon.

There were eleven of us on our walk to-day. There are now five Jehovah's Witnesses here, including a man and wife. The wife lives next to me (on the other side we have a Jew again). We cannot agree with all the ideas of these people. They teach much which does not seem to me to be from the Bible; they have many strange teachings about the end of the world and most of them, although not all, have left the Church. They are, however, a living reproach to us that we have neglected the teaching of the Last Things. They see many things, in their own way, much clearer and much better than the majority of Church-Christians. . . .

COBLENZ, 16th November, 1937 (Unofficial)

I have now informed the Gestapo, in writing, of my attitude to the affair of the sermon notes. . . . Do not forget the kingdom of God in all the duties and burdens of our home. We must learn to give up and to forget

D

much; but we must not throw away the sausage with the skin! As much is lost, let us take even in our loss this blessing: 'Cast thy bread upon the waters and thou shalt receive it after many days. . . .'

COBLENZ, 17th November, 1937 (Unofficial)

A short greeting to you on the evening of Repentance Day. It has been a day of rich blessing with God's Word. I have, in a real sense, felt the power of gentleness, love and patience, and, so far as I am able, I have let go all desire for profit in life and office. God grant that I may profit truly from all the digging and fertilizing of the vineyard and that I may bring forth fruit in my office and in my Church and also in my family.

COBLENZ, 23rd November, 1937 (Unofficial)

I am to be fined and it is well known that I shall refuse to pay the fine. My fine is because of the stand I have taken in common with the Confessing Church and, because it is known that I will not pay, I am being held like a bailiff in the house of a debtor—except that I am the debtor! Herr O. intended to be cynical when he informed me that I was to be fined again, but he at least admitted that my imprisonment so far had been a punishment. He thought that perhaps I would hesitate when I realized how much you would suffer at home. I said, they can do what they like; they know well that, in every way, I considered my imprisonment to be unjust. Read Isaiah 10, which I have specially noted: God's righteous anger against the proud Assyrians, who knew not that they were only the rod of God's judgment against his people Israel. For Israel's God had 'found as a nest the riches of the people'; and as one gathers eggs, he would plunder their nests and destroy them. 'Shall the axe boast itself against him that heweth therewith? or shall the saw magnify itself against him that shaketh it? as if the rod should shake itself against them that lift it up, or as if the staff should lift up itself, as if it were no wood.' Israel's light will be as a fire and her holiness as a flame to burn up and destroy the power of Assyria, until the trees of the forest be so few that a child could count them. The remnant of Israel shall be purified by the fire of God's judgment. Therefore, Israel shall no longer be afraid of Assyria. For the Lord will deal with Assyria as he dealt with the Egyptians. Oppression will come, but when the troubles are greatest, then God will send help—the power of Assyria will be brought to nought in Israel.

COBLENZ, 24th November, 1937

Now, as we thought, the dice have been thrown. It is to be either a concentration camp or a prison camp. It matters little which. We are delivered into their hands and must expect the treatment of men, with all that entails. You must see to it that our church remains independent. I cannot understand why I am so suddenly to be transferred to a camp. I suppose all decisions taken here are already decided in higher places and are, therefore, simply the carrying out of orders. Now, what should I advise you to do? Viewed from outside, that is easy enough. I can see already that the time is coming when every true Christian will have to stand up openly for his faith, making a clear decision and an open confession. You will very soon have your whole attention directed towards the preserving of our children and already you are called to a decision. Then think of these words: 'It is better to lose all creatures than to find yourself fighting against the will of God', and put your trust in his promise: 'Who fears God has a sure hiding

place and his children also will be sheltered.' Let us not
take the tragic way of so many unfaithful Christian
parents. Keep our people true—God will give you the
power, my dearest, to hold fast on this way. Before you
ask advice of men, seek it of God. For even the best of
our friends will give us bad counsel at times. The people
of Buchenwald will become my people, as near to my
heart as those who have become my people in Coblenz.
Mr and Mrs M., from O., are travelling with me, by the
same transport. Apparently, I am to be in the same camp
as Mr M., so I shall be with the 'sectarians'. We shall
certainly serve one another. Mrs M. is now, after her
bad illness, quite well and peaceful.

Give my greetings to the brethren. We shall not count
our lives dear when the wolf attacks the sheep, greedy
for the souls of our people and especially for our young
people. We shall not be found wanting when the wolf
comes. Where there is an hireling, the wolf catcheth and
scattereth the sheep. Let us remember, dearest, that our
light afflictions, which are but temporal, work for us
an exceeding weight of glory, which is for eternity. Our
children belong to God through our faith and their
baptism in Christ. The true Lord will care for them in
soul and body.

Paul wrote a farewell note to the children, to our helper
in the house and also to the assistant, Vikar Kemper. In
the last of these, he said : ' When you greet the brethren
for me, tell them in all things to do God's will and to
walk uprightly before the people. Tell them to spring
into the yawning breach and, into this battle, let them
throw all that is most dear to them. A breach has surely
been torn in our lives by the frightful seduction and
idolatry of the spirit of our day. This must be repaired.
Prudence and cleverness will get us nowhere. Behold the
company of cautious ministers in their churches! In

his battle we must wager our lives or else nothing is
won.'

Then came the day when the post brought one of the
usual postcards from Paul. Again, it was the jailor who
had informed him, earlier than the official notification,
which transport would take him to the concentration
camp. He also had forwarded the postcard to me. The
card was dated 23rd November 1937 and bore on the
postmark the time—10 p.m. It read: 'How lovely it
would be if we could meet again, before the transport
takes me away from here at noon on Thursday. Herr O.
has said that he would bear in mind an application for
permission to see me before I leave. As we have done,
we shall leave all in God's hands, trusting him with
patience and courage. From him alone can we expect
all good things. Him shall we love with all our heart
and him alone shall we fear and worship. So shall God
be with us and our hope will not make us ashamed. Be
of good cheer, be true and fear not. I hold you fast in
my heart. In God we are not divided. Thank you for all
the love you have given me. We shall give thanks for
this time of preparation, making us ready for new trials.
New sufferings should bring us new experiences of our
God and new glory. Christ said: 'Lo, I am with you
alway'. . . . Food, and money also, I suppose, cannot
be taken with us to the camp. Other things can be sent
in to us. I need a fresh pair of socks. My greetings to
you all. In love, your Paul.'

As I was ready to leave for Coblenz, the telephone
rang with the welcome news that I had permission to
speak with my husband once again. That made the third
time the jailor had got permission for me—bless him!

Next morning, Paul and I were together again. A few
days before, he had managed to get from the Gestapo all
his prison letters for June and July. These letters had
been a great comfort to him. For my part, I held on

to the text: 'For whom the Lord loveth, he chasteneth
and scourgeth every son whom he receiveth.' We talked
of this. As it was the Friday before Advent, I had an
Advent *Kranz*[1] with me. Paul took it with him and, by
the light of the candles, he read the Advent hymns later
in his cell. Paul knew that this day he could be free if
only he would pledge himself to accept and obey the
order of banishment. Our hearts were heavy. I touched
Paul gently and said, 'How much I love you!' He
was deeply moved, even to tears. We said no more. The
Officer made it clear to us that we had little time and
would soon have to go. Falteringly, we prayed the
Lord's Prayer together. I gave to Paul the text for the
day: 'The lion of Judah shall break every chain.' Our
time was up. But, at that moment, a grief-stricken man
was led away and the disturbance gave us more time
together. The man was utterly shattered. He was not the
last to be seen like that. Paul and I held on to each
other. We dare not express our feelings too gently. The
Advent hymns were our comfort and Paul repeated
them. We then talked of everyday things. The jailor
joined in our conversation and we even wandered to the
point of talking about heavy artillery! In the same room
with us were the Jehovah's Witnesses—husband and
wife—also saying good-bye. Both of them were going to
concentration camps. The woman came over and shook
my hand: 'It's hard', she said, 'we owe so much to
your husband for his comfort and encouragement. God
bless you!'

My last sight of Paul was in the prison lorry. He went
away from me smiling.

[1] The little wreath of pine twigs set up in every home and
church during Advent. For each Sunday in Advent a candle is
added to the wreath and lit.

VIII

CONCENTRATION CAMP

ON ADVENT Sunday, 1937, the church was deeply moved. The assistant preached from Psalm 130. The people stood firmly behind their pastor. All that winter members of the congregation came to our home to pray every evening for him. As summer came, we did not continue this evening time of prayer, perhaps because of extra work and the more difficult political situation, but we kept the weekly service of intercession. The following winter, we organized the regular services of the church again and had learnt, as far as possible, to do what Paul would have done. Meanwhile, we used every means we could to appeal for Paul's release. All to no avail. Paul was an enemy of the State.

News of him came to me from many quarters. I heard of his faithful witness, of his pastoral work, of the great comfort he had been to many. In my mind, I could picture 'The Pastor of Buchenwald'. His letters told the story of his inner life. Here is a selection from them.

BUCHENWALD, 29th November, 1937

You will be anxious to have news of me. We arrived here on Saturday morning. My first impressions are, therefore, over. Like all beginnings they were hard. I no longer feel lonely in my cell; but I am more than ever thankful for the transition period at Coblenz. I have, so to speak, been let into this gradually. With God's help, both of us, you too at home, will be happy and faithful during this time of preparation for Christmas. This year, above all, we shall receive the deep inner joy of Advent and Christmas, which is quite independent of outward circumstances. We must accept the joy of this season. Especially at home you must rejoice, lest our children or strangers look for our joy and find only sorrow. I beg you to do this as I shall also try to do. Let us rejoice at God's gift. We know full well that our fate is in God's hands.

Let me get back to the beginning of this letter. I am quite well. It is important to be healthy in this place and I am thankful to God for the good constitution which he gave me. It was lovely to see you in Coblenz before I left. It hurt, of course, to say good-bye to you; but now the memory of it makes up for all the hurt. In the difficult days that lie ahead, my dear, true wife will be a strength to me. Thank you for walking with me and for the courage you have shown in the way you must walk now alone. Your way is not an easy one any more than mine is. Be sure of my love and my prayers for all of you.

BUCHENWALD, 5th December, 1937

Now, I am coming to your Sunday letter, a habit which I must not lose. As you see, I am not used to writing these days. Thank God I have my first week behind me. I thank him also that at the end of the week I am still sound and well. I hope that, by now, you have received my first letter which told you of my first impressions. I also hope that I shall receive some word from you during the next week. You will understand that, despite the fellowship of many fellow-prisoners, I can still feel lonely at times. But the good God is with me here and can make that which is 'far off', 'near'. He can make this strange land my homeland. He can meet me, in this world, with all the power of the world that is to come. I know that this is what you pray for me.

Now, as Christmas approaches, the little children will be getting excited, more and more every day, and you will all sing the Advent hymns with enthusiasm. Yes, these hymns have a special meaning for us and their promises take on a new life.

> And ye, beneath life's crushing load
> Whose forms are bending low,
> Who toil along the climbing way
> With painful steps and slow.

Therein we see ourselves. He will not fail you either. Look up! ' as the hymn says. I know the troubles I have brought upon you, with no father at home and all that entails. If dark clouds seem to overshadow the glorious festival that lies before you, 'Look up'. The eternal light, which lit up the poor manger at Bethlehem, would find a way into our darkened hearts. It will purify our hearts and overcome the darkness. Separated though we are, we shall keep the feast, with trust and faith. For God can give us joy, even in these times. Little kindnesses and helps come to me even here and lighten my life.

BUCHENWALD, 9th January, 1938

I am sorry that circumstances have so spoiled our correspondence that you did not receive my Christmas letter and that your birthday passed without a special greeting from me. I am sorry, but there was nothing I could do. Now, I must tell you of what is happening to me. I am still sound and healthy. I am beginning to get myself adjusted to this place. I have received three letters from you. The first came at the end of the second

week here. The Christmas letter came on Christmas Eve.
To see your dear handwriting and to know that we
faced the joy of Christmas together, despite our separation, was more to me than all the other greetings that
many sent to me. I am grateful for those others and
they are dear to me; but yours was more precious than
anything I have ever received. Your third letter came on
7th January. How happy I was to hear that you had
kept the feast with true faith and joy, and that you had
been blessed! How I longed to be with you and with our
dear friends!

BUCHENWALD, 23rd January, 1938

Your dear letter of the 18th January came on Friday.
How good it is that even when our letters seem to be
cut off, we still hold fast together in faith and trust in
God and are kept from burning sorrow. Disappointed,
we often are, but not unto despair. I am glad that you
went to Berlin. You would be surrounded by fine people
and find interest in the journey. But now you are home
and that will be a greater joy to you. The Lord is very
good to us. I was especially pleased to hear that our
children are well. Healthy, obedient, industrious and
good—that is fine news! Distance may separate us, but
I can feel my love for you from this great distance.
Every evening, I am beside your bed in my imagination.
Especially I thought of you on your birthday. I am glad
to hear that you were given so helpful a text and word
of comfort in Dahlem on your birthday. Thank you for
the texts in your last letter. They have helped me much.
Perhaps you could send me the texts for the next two
Sundays and one or other of the readings selected. In
this way, we can be reading and thinking upon the same
passage and be closely bound together in prayer.
    There is not much news from here; but I can quite

honestly say that I am still well and am almost beginning to make myself at home! Here, too, we may thank
God for work and food, which we receive from his
hand. Here, too, God makes the 23rd Psalm come true.
He restores our soul, he leads us in the paths of
righteousness for his name's sake. Above all, we will
hold fast to the promise of God, that he will lead out
the prisoners in his own good time, and we shall possess
our souls in patience.

BUCHENWALD, 6th February, 1938

At noon to-day, I received your dear letter, written on
the 2nd of this month. How glad and thankful I am for
this good news. . . . It is clear to us now, my darling,
and the knowledge gives me great gladness that, despite
all our sins against our love, yet all the storms and
shocks have only bound us closer together. This, I think,
is because, despite all our failures, we have really tried
to fear God above all things, to love him and to trust
him. This we have learnt to do in Jesus Christ, his
beloved Son, our Lord. Thus, my bond which holds me
to you, bound like a bunch of grapes to the vine, and
my bond with all our dear family is not a burden, but
a strength. I am not alone and that strengthens me to
follow my ordained path. I have complete confidence
that God's good Spirit, which keeps us while we are
separated, will lead us further in the way that we must
tread and that the eye of God will mark our paths. . . .

Once again, all the news I have is to say thankfully
that I am well. I think you would approve if you saw
how well I looked. The long periods in the open air
make me look very well indeed. So far, God has led me
kindly and kept me from all illness and accident. His
care for us all is truly wonderful and he gently leads
us out.

Little Gerhard will now have had his birthday. He enters his new year of life with very much to learn. I am sure he will learn in this coming year to be strong and brave, as well as obedient. How much I wanted to be with you on his birthday and all last Tuesday I tried to picture you at home. The table would be arrayed for him and you would all sing his song. I wanted to sing my greetings with you.

BUCHENWALD, 20th February, 1938

I know you are anxious about me and I wish I had more news to give you. So little happens here that I can write about. Be content to know that I am still well. The winter cold has done me no harm. Even my leg is getting better. I am able to exercise it much more now that I am out working. Sundays, of course, are special days and we look forward to them all week. Then my thoughts and prayers blend with yours and we are together at the throne of grace. Not only on Sundays, but especially then. I read with you the same lines of Scripture and comment which you have sent to me. The reminder of you is a sweet sorrow. Each night, as I go to bed and thank God that he has given to me a warm camp, gradually the longing for home steals upon me. I am no longer brave. . . .

As you write to me of all the winter games the children are enjoying, I join with them in their joy. Remember how we used to ski and especially our accident at Müller's. Remember how we swept down the hillside into a watery grave. What fun we had! What pleasure we had in the glorious snowy landscape!

It is a great comfort to me that you have found a friend in Irmgaard. God has truly given you many fine people to keep you from loneliness and to make up, in some measure, for our separation. How kind the Lord is! . . . I am very proud to hear that my big son makes his way alone to school and takes his place there. What a young man he has become!

BUCHENWALD, 6th March, 1938

Yes, you are right. Here, too, the frost and the snow have gone and the signs of spring are breaking in upon us. We rejoice at warmer sun, the sound of the birds in the trees and all the stirring of new life. It does body and soul good. We are happy despite everything. So, with great thankfulness, I can write again and tell you that I am still well. Above all we can be glad and thankful that our letters keep open the life-line between us. There are things we cannot write, but we hold these even more firmly in faith. These are the unfulfilled longings that only we understand. Unspoken and unwritten they hold us yet closer together. They are the many little things, which Claudius recalls in his lovely evening hymn, 'the things we laugh about' or perhaps cry about, 'because our eyes see them not'. There are also things we cannot say and may not know, but simply leave God to order as he will.

Pray for me that I may be a true follower of our crucified Lord and that I may witness a good confession in this time of testing. During this Passiontide, may I follow him closely. For you, too, I pray that, with our people, you may be blessed this Passiontide.

You will be glad to be at work again in the garden.

BUCHENWALD, 23rd March, 1938

At last I have had word from you again. It is your letter of the 16th of this month. Thank you for it. I am still well. We are glad of the warm, dry March days, which suit me fine. You will be hard at work in the garden. In my mind's eye, I can see you there with all the children helping.

Where I sleep now is near to an open window. The moon and the stars shine through to me in a friendly way and are as a parable, even messengers, of that other light which shines into our darkness. By the light which comes from God, those who sit in the darkness and sorrow of this world shall be lightened. . . . Especially in the early morning, when I wake, I think of you. I think of your concerns, the uncertainty of your daily needs, the sorrow and the work. Yet I know that God's true hand will care for you and you shall lack nothing.

Please kiss our dear six for their father.

BUCHENWALD, 4th April, 1938

How glad I am always to be able to tell you that all goes well with me and that I am sound in body and soul. We had such a lovely spring and March was so unexpectedly fine that surely we have no more to fear from the cold winds of winter. They are passed. Winter has been conquered and summer stands waiting at the door.

As we celebrate the resurrection of our Lord, we celebrate the victory of life over death. Our faith is the victory which overcometh the world. When I think on your troubles and your work, I make one simple petition: that you may be given new power and new faith. Your troubles lie also upon our children. Let us all take our anxieties and our troubles and lay them upon him who is able to bear them better than we are. I wonder if our youngest, who is born into such a troublous world, will eventually know a world of far greater peace? Will Dietrich find his way in this world? Oh, the questions that crowd in upon us! But leave this to our God. Let the joy which our children bring to you

be ever a source of power and help. Rejoice in them.
How lovely it will be when we see each other again!
Who knows how soon that might be? How we shall
rejoice in each other! God knows the way and he knows
what we have yet to suffer and what joy lies ahead for
us. How is Mother bearing up under these burdens?
Greet her for me with true and thankful love.

BUCHENWALD, Easter, 1938

As in the last few days, Easter itself has come to us in
a rough and unfriendly way with April showers. I mean
the weather, not Easter itself. Even the weather has
recanted a little, for a few rays of sunshine pierced the
clouds for a moment to tell us of coming glory. That is
true in more senses than one: I am thankful for the
quickening of body and soul, which comes with these
rays of sunshine. In all my trials, that quickening has
come to me, that promise of future glory. Truly it comes
from our Father in heaven. I am thankful for your love
and for the rich memories and for your Easter prayer. I
was very happy to have your long letter of the 1st of
April. Even from here, I seem to be able to see how well
our two gardens are flourishing under your careful
hands, each in their own way. It is a great joy and satisfaction to know that the teacher has given our children
good reports.
It is Easter and we are spurred on to attain our risen
life. That great gift waits to grow out of this life of
death. It can grow and the way is the way of faith, faith
given to us by God. For when we talk of faith, it is God
with whom we have to deal. We may indeed be thankful that, in the midst of all our sorrow, we are at peace.
The exalted message and the spur to faith which is in
this Christian festival leads us to true joy and happiness.
For Christians, these outer things are not to be compared

with the glory that shall be. Comfort, reputation, outward happiness are all cheap substitutes for the true glory.

I do not need to assure you any more that I am well. Let us pursue our way with patience and peaceful trust. I shall try to endure patiently the absence of news and leave in God's hands the care of my church. His hands are true and gentle.

Always give to the children father's kiss.

The last paragraph of that letter tells of Paul's sad acceptance of the censorship, which was now to be much stricter and to keep from him much news he dearly loved to hear.

The clash came in April 1938. While Paul was free, he could avoid saluting the Nazi flag, but in the concentration camp it was different. He had never saluted the Swastika because he saw it, not only as a symbol of the authority which ruled the land, but as a symbol of an ideology which he utterly rejected. Whether it was on his way to work, as the officer reported, or whether he was informed on by other prisoners, or whether he refused on some official occasion, we do not clearly know. Probably all these things happened. Paul simply refused to salute the flag and was taken to the punishment cell. He stayed there almost continuously for fourteen months. He was handed over to the mercy and cruelty of SS Leader Sommer. In his last days, Paul freely denounced this man before the other prisoners as a murderer and a tyrant. Something of Paul's suffering is summed up by the clerk, Herr Leikam, who was with him in Buchenwald. Here is part of that material:

' In the spring of 1938, there was an order that all prisoners passing by the Nazi flag on their march to work should greet it by taking off their caps. Schneider declared that this saluting of the Nazi flag was idolatry and he refused to obey the order. At first, most of the prisoners did not think of refusing. None of them did it willingly; but, apart from Schneider, they all obeyed. One who envied him, or perhaps had a grudge against him, informed the authorities and he was charged with refusal to obey a command. Then began Paul Schneider's lone path of suffering. He was called to the SS and freely confessed his attitude. At first he received twenty-five lashes and was then put into the dark cell. This meant solitary confinement and he remained in this cell till his death. There he told the SS exactly what the Christian attitude to Nazism was. He spoke freely and without fear. There was probably no other man in Germany who denounced the régime as fearlessly. He called the devil by his name: murderer, criminal, tyrant, monster. Because of this witness against Nazism, and he never failed to set against it the grace of Christ and call men to repentance, Schneider received in his body repeated and heavy tortures, humiliations and pains. All the ingenuity of Nazi sadism was used against him. Torture was alternated with good treatment and appeals to relax his strong opposition. Schneider was unmoved and he was tireless in calling out words of Scripture to his fellow-prisoners. Morning and evening, whenever his cell door was opened or he was taken out to fresh torment, his voice could be heard shouting aloud words of comfort and judgment from the Bible. . . . One January morning in 1939, when two escaped prisoners had been brought back and killed, Paul Schneider could be heard clearly denouncing the murder: 'In the name of Jesus Christ, I witness against the murder of prisoners. . . .' The worst time for Schneider was in the early summer of 1939. For several days he was hung up, with his hands behind him and his body permanently bent. This devilish device caused him continuous pain. His suffering was borne nobly and he was greatly honoured in the camp. We saw in him the meaning of the words: "My bonds in Christ are manifest in all the palace." '

But why was Paul never released from his punishment cell? Many other prisoners were put into such confinement for shorter or longer terms, but also came out again to return to their work, or they were released by death. He was their pastor and him they feared the most. Many of his fellow prisoners have since told me of his memorable resistance.

He was permitted occasional letters, even from the punishment cell, and these I have preserved with special care. The final chapter reproduces some of them. They were all written under the growing certainty that he could find no release in this life.

IX

LETTERS FROM
THE PUNISHMENT CELL

15th May, 1938

Now, at last, I can turn to that which means so much
to both of us, our letters. Thank you for all the good
news you gave me in your two letters of 13th April
and 4th May, which I have now received. The news has
gladdened me, as it gave me one more sign of the con-
tinuing love of God. . . . The terrible weather which
we had at the turn of the month would itself make you
feel gloomy. Now that is over. I was glad to hear of the
buds bursting and the shoots coming through the earth
in our garden. How glad that will make you! The cold
weather at the end of April must have delayed them and
you feel they had forgotten to come. Our earthly
gardens are like that. For all our sowing and planting,
we cannot hurry them forward. It is wise for us not to
set our hearts too much on our earthly gardens, lest we
forget the garden of our soul. It is this garden which
must be made ready for the kingdom of God and, with
all diligence, we must set the fruits of the Spirit in it.
More care and patience is needed for this garden than for
our earthly garden.

Now the May sun is shining and it is warm again. All
around us, even Buchenwald, is clothed in its beauty.
Like you in your garden and our farmers in their fields,
I too can be glad at the coming of the sunshine.

The care which Irmgaard Humburg has shown you

115

in your troubles has moved me. I am deeply grateful to her for her sisterly help and I rejoice that the distance between Barmen and Hunsrueck has become so short-ened. As husband and father, I long for you all and am sometimes troubled within; but this comfort of men helps to still my troubles.

[In this letter, Paul Schneider is saying as clearly as he may, through the censorship, that he is grateful to the Confessing Church for standing by his family.]

19th June, 1938

Because of a misunderstanding, which has led to my present circumstances, I have not been able to write to you since my letter of 15th May. You must forgive me, so far as I am guilty, for this sorrow which I have brought upon you. At least now I can assure you that I am still alive and well. For the future, we must trust the gracious and wonderful care of our God. We must also be ready at all times to find in him a substitute for our human love. Yet he is more than a substitute! For-give me if my clumsy words bring you sorrow. I am so conscious of the poverty of my love. You and the children deserved better. You should have had kindness, sunshine and love: It is left to others to give you these. Enough of this. Let me thank you for your letter of May 19th and for the later one. Not least was I gladdened to hear of the children and other personal news. I hope that Mariele will soon be there to help you, if she has not already come. Please don't send any more money. Pray for me that I may hold fast to the right path.

13th July, 1938

Because my circumstances have not much changed, I have had to wait until to-day before I could answer your two letters. I have just received the one you wrote on the 7th of this month. Thank you for all the joy and strength these letters give to me. You must not think that things are going badly with me here. I am all right. If you saw me now, you would be quite satisfied with my appearance. I don't look haggard and drawn or underfed. I am still given the strength to face what every day brings and whatever courage I have is due to your constant prayers for me and also the prayers of others. How well I can remember a year ago and with what joy I think of it! Remember how God gave to us that day our sixth child. What a happy day it was and how we enjoyed our holiday together at B.B. and E. with the children! We shall not forget that. We shall remember what a precious thing it is to have this joy and hold it with patience through all adversity. Then we shall see that even this time of separation, which cannot last much longer, will be for the best. We are already beginning to see that in part. I am as happy as you are that our house has helped again to bring two people together in love. Neither can I think of anybody to whom I would rather lose our dear Tutti than to our good 'uncle' (this was Paul's pet name for his assistant and successor, Leo Kemper). Yet we are not losing her. She will still be ours. It will be your concern, as a good mother-in-law, to see that they really get to know each other and then to get them married as soon as you can! Their love will find its fulfilment in true marriage. They should have no difficulty in finding a house in Womrath. My blessing on them. My heartfelt wishes flow out to them.

And all the other things you have written make me as happy as if I were there. Convey my thanks for all the greetings of friends from near and far.

12th August, 1938

Outwardly we come to the 12th anniversary of ou
wedding bitterly separated and with grief and sorrow
Yet, in spirit and in faith we are closer bound togethe
than ever before. Therefore, let us be thankful an
rejoice in God. As I am writing this, you will already
be on your journey with the children and Leo.
thoroughly approve of your plan to drink deep of th
old Dickenschied air. There is nothing like your hom
air to give you life again. You need it, with all the care
of a mother. I hope your duties are not going to be to
heavy. May God guide you to-day, give you a happy
arrival, and may your holidays be fine and richly blessed
To your mother and your dear relatives, I am deeply
grateful that they have made this holiday possible.
hope it will help you to enjoy your holiday to know
that nothing has altered here and that I can truly say
that all goes well with me. I have very little work t
do and am quite sound and well.

21st September, 1938

I was very glad to have your letter of 8th Septembe
on the 14th, shortly after I had answered your letter o
9th August. I know that you have been thinking of m
on my birthday and I want to say 'thank you' for al
your love. Now our little baby, under the care an
blessing of God, must learn to walk out into life. Yo
must teach him to walk when his little legs are stron
enough. Sadly, I think that you must do it alone. Littl
Evemarie is already nine years old. I thought of her o
1st September and knew how happy she would be whe
she discovered her flute. I pictured her joy. Our goo
shepherd will give her a happy year of life and guid
her in all her ways, at play and at school. How happy

I will be when I first see my babies again! Already they are becoming strange to me and my little daughter is growing up. I hope Dieter will soon be vying with Eve-marie to play the flute. Then we shall hear some fine music. I am sorry to hear about Sophie. She must take care of herself and rest.

Don't worry too much about the long intervals between these letters. You know I am in good hands. I am still sound and well.

4th October, 1938

It is now exactly a year since, after that lovely holi-day, we were once again separated. We knew that this time it would be serious and long. How hard this separation is, we are now beginning to learn. But we shall be brave and continue on this way, because we know that we are led by God. Perhaps we are very soon to learn the blessing which comes out of affliction, when we are once again united. For then I shall be a much better and a much more loving husband. Above all we have learnt that this temporal separation leads to an eternal union. I last wrote to you fourteen days ago. Nothing has changed and I am well. What has happened to you since your holiday in Dickenschied? My sugges-tion to Leo, that he should marry soon, was meant quite seriously. They are old enough and they have enough to live on. They have their faith. Greetings from my heart to all our dear ones and especially to the two sweethearts, I am confident that our God will make up to the tiniest of our children all that they are missing by my absence—and he will make it up richly. How I long to play with my little ones! I think on you, my dear, with deep affection.

18th October, 1938

Thank you with all my heart for your dear letter which came the day before yesterday as a true Sabbath joy. How glad I am that things are going much better with you now and that so many satisfactory changes have taken place in the home. It is good to read that even the heavy burdens seem light again. It is a great comfort to me here to know that I have such dear and such industrious children. How vividly I can see, in my mind's eye, the potato field, with all the little children and the womenfolk and the machine in-between! Baked potatoes will taste twice as good after such a day's work! . . . I was glad to read what you said about Luise. How did they manage to find the darling so quickly? . . . I understand, dearest, what you write about this time of waiting. It is painful to you, also, I know. I hope the letter which has since gone to you from me will bring you a little comfort. We must be thankful and glad that, after more than a year, I am still well and sound and that, so far, I can still send greetings to you with gladness and comfort. Whatever comes, we have this promise: it cannot be heavier than we can bear. God knows the right time for everything. He knows the time of growth and the time of harvest. And this, not only for the fruit of the field, but also for our lives—our own harvest and growth.

20th March, 1939

How glad I am that I can write to you again and show you some sign of life! God be praised and thanked! I am still well and, from your one letter of 17th February,[1] I take it that you are, too. How I have thanked God for that one letter! This long silence, with

[1] All my other letters were returned to me.

no news from one to another, has been hard for you to
bear as it has been for me and our sorrows have been
the same. We have travelled a good deal further along
the way of separation and affliction. I have worried a
great deal over Dieter, who is growing up now, and I
am glad to have news of how you have dealt with the
danger to him. It was a good solution of the problem.[2]
My greetings and thanks to the Lutzes for helping us in
this way, and to the boy himself.

How many festivals have we kept during the past half
year, bound together in spirit and, therefore, keeping the
feast together! I hope that your praise and thanks and
joy have not failed on these great festivals, even when
your heart was sore to breaking—my dear love. We
shall not let the time be too long. You know the old
story of one who served seven years for his loved one,
and yet seven years more; but the years seemed to him
like weeks for the love he bore to her. So may our love
be to one another and may the greatest love we know
shorten the time of our affliction. One day, we shall be
free. That day surely comes.

Postcard dated 5th April, 1939

A truly blessed and happy Easter to you and to all our
friends. A good holiday to our big boy. He will be a
comfort to his mother and you will be glad that he is
nearer to you for a while. Our 'Dicker' will be home
again and, for the first time, he will be able to search
for the Easter hare with 'Goldiger'. Uncle will be
hiding the Easter eggs for the children to find. I have
now received the letter of 16th March.

[2] From January 1939, Dieter lived with Pastor Lutze in Barmen.
There he could attend the Elberfeld School and escape member-
ship of the Hitler Youth.

Postcard dated 9th May, 1939

Your letter of 25th April was my Easter letter. Thank you. I know now how you kept the feast and I know of your Coblenz journey. I am glad of all the life and comfort which is so strong around you. My sincere greetings and thanks to the friends who have been so good to you. Dieter carries into his new year of life a father's blessing and best wishes. His progress is a comfort and a joy to me. Especial thanks to the Lutzes for all their goodness. Let us with patience and confidence wait for the right outcome of this our separation.

8th June, 1939

Your Whitsun letter was again a 'children' letter and I was glad. Thank you. Especially I was glad to see the greetings, written with their own hands. I can see from these how much they have learnt and how much they have grown. Time here seems to stand still. I shall have to see what presents to bring for the children when I return. Your letter has really made me feel as though I am away on holiday and must soon begin to think what to bring back as presents for the children I am afraid that there is no such chance of chocolate! Yes, my dearest, the 'children' letter has done me good I shall treasure it. Your continued watch over our six dear ones, your love and care for them, will help them to face the future bravely and erect. That is to be a great comfort. They are the pledge of our love, rooted and grounded in the truth of God, and they will help us Their very growth and soundness tells us that our love does not fail. When the troubles come and we 'pass through the waters', our love is held by the strong tie of those six pledges. You have given me hope again. I too, believe that the wound which now sorely distresses our family will one day be healed. The children will not grow away from their father. Let us, therefore, fortify our patience anew.

I know nothing of the plans for Leo's and Tutti's wedding. They must get on with it and not wait for me to return. Our dear uncle cannot go on acting as 'deputy father' to our family. He has his own to build. He must build it unencumbered. It will be in everybody's interest to go ahead with the arrangements. We do not know what the future holds or how things will turn out.

For my part, I have had a happy and blessed Whitsun. The spirit of God 'bloweth where it listeth'. I am well. Please do not worry too much about me.

18th June, 1939

It was foolish of me in my last letter to place our very human hopes so high that I seemed to forget that God's ways, which are not always the same as our hopes, are just and holy and for our salvation. We must have but one hope, 'the living hope'. That hope, we must learn again every day. That hope must be our only wish. We must follow our Lord.

The Last Letter

This letter, which was sent on 3rd July, 1939, was the last Paul Schneider wrote before his death and Frau Schneider has published it without any omissions. The personal references and greetings, which are often cut from the other letters, are left in this precious 'last word'.

MY DEAR GRETEL,

On the day before yesterday, I received your dear letter from Oberstdorf with greetings from

Sophie, Mariele and the four warriors. Many thanks for the letter and for all the greetings. I am so glad that, thanks to the kindness of friends, you can enjoy these lovely days of holiday with Evemarie, as a little compensation for all your difficulties. Thanks also to Mariele, who has taken your place at home. How kind is God's care and guidance! Our little daughter's already in the mountains. Perhaps mother too will soon be well and strong, climbing mountains! I hope the weather keeps good for you. It was lovely thirteen years ago (i.e. on our honeymoon). God allowed us to have one more trip to the south, for one holiday together. The many visits will keep our house busy and help you to pass this difficult time more easily. My greetings to Leo and his parents. I always remember Herbert Mayer as a man of trust. Greet him for me. It is a good and very satisfactory arrangement for the young couple to live with you—for the time being! Thank them for this sacrifice. Mother will take the parting from Conrad hard. What a pity she cannot come to us, that our little house is not big enough. How pushed about she is in her old age! 'My time is restlessness . . .' If only we could learn from all this and mature by that which is come to us and overcome the sorrows! Now, I wish this letter could get to you as quickly as yours came to me. Greet your kind hosts with my thankfulness. May God richly bless you and our dear little daughter during these days of holiday and may you have a happy homecoming.

Yours,

PAUL

That was the last letter. I returned from Oberstdorf with little Evemarie on 14th July. The next day, we were beset with visits because of the departure of our assistant pastor. He was called for military service on 18th July. This delayed our morning prayers, which we held between 10 and 11 a.m. Our text was, 'Man looketh on the outward appearance, but the Lord looketh on the heart.' The hymn we sang, 'O Thou who breakest every band', was a great strength to me in the next few days. In the evening, at 6.30, I received the telegram: 'Paul Schneider, born 29th August, 1897, died to-day. If it is wished to bury at own cost, contact within 24 hours, Registrar of deaths, Weimar. Otherwise, cremation. Camp Commandant, Buchenwald.' That night, I went to Weimar.

Paul Schneider was buried at Dickenschied, 21st July, 1939. His grave became a memorial and a strength to the Confessing Church, whose struggle with Hitler was to go on for six years of war. Karl Barth spoke for many when he wrote in a letter dated 3rd August, 1939, less than two weeks after the funeral:

'He is delivered, his faith has become sight, he has gone home. The crown of life crowns the true man even in death. His faithful witness has helped many to do and say what is right and God has honoured him in allowing him to suffer. The New Testament speaks of this honour of suffering. It is not for nothing. It is a signpost, pointing up higher, where honour is given and the crown of life will be received.'

SCRIPTURE REFERENCES

NAMES AND SUBJECTS

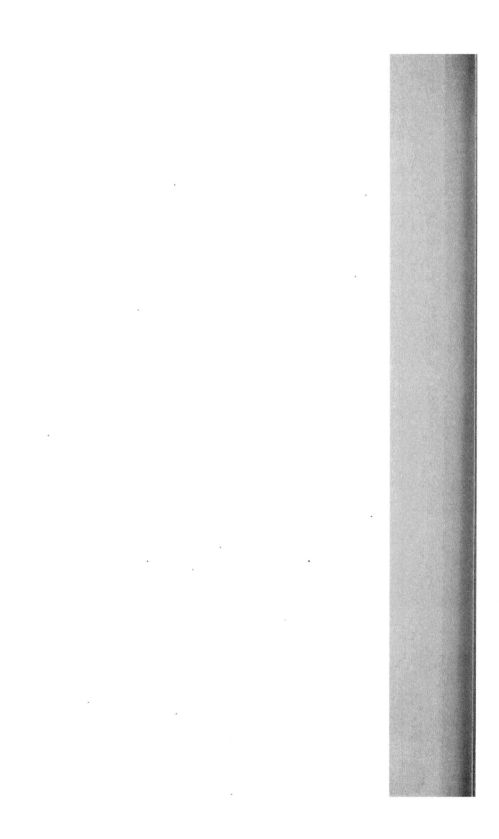

CPSIA information can be obtained
at www.ICGtesting.com
Printed in the USA
BVHW051552130223
658395BV00002B/40